T0393163

Urban Density Contextualized

Urban Density Contextualized provides planners with the tools to understand, assess, and implement urban density successfully.

It systematically explores the social context of urban density, and how it plays a role in urban design and planning strategies. Cities and places have unique cultures and identities, and a wide range of considerations need to be considered in the attempt to insert more density. This book acknowledges this relationship—between urban density and social and physical context—and investigates the ways in which density can use this context to enhance livability and promote a more sustainable world. Chapters include the following topics: density and housing, accessibility, affordability, zoning, typology, and history, as well as case studies of design strategy from across the U.S.

It is essential for urban planners, architects, landscape architects, and others working in design and planning fields.

Sungduck Lee is Assistant Professor in the Department of Design Innovation at the University of Minnesota, with a background in urban design and urbanism. Her research and teaching interest lies at the intersection of social geography and visual communication. She directs the Geosocial Visualization Research Lab that explores various social characteristics of communities, and their relationship to geospatial context.

Emily Talen is Professor of Urbanism at the University of Chicago, where she teaches urban design and directs the Urbanism Lab. Her previous books include *New Urbanism and American Planning*; *Design for Diversity, Urban Design Reclaimed*; *City Rules*; *Neighborhood*; and *What Cities Say*.

Urban Density Contextualized

Design Strategies for Building Density in Cities

Sungduck Lee and Emily Talen

Routledge
Taylor & Francis Group

NEW YORK AND LONDON

Designed cover image: Sungduck Lee

First published 2025
by Routledge
605 Third Avenue, New York, NY 10158

and by Routledge
4 Park Square, Milton Park, Abingdon, Oxon, OX14 4RN

Routledge is an imprint of the Taylor & Francis Group, an informa business

© 2025 Sungduck Lee and Emily Talen

Library of Congress Cataloging-in-Publication Data
Names: Lee, Sungduck, author. | Talen, Emily, 1958– author.
Title: Urban density contextualized: design strategies for building density in
cities / Sungduck Lee and Emily Talen.
Description: New York, NY: Routledge, 2025. |
Includes bibliographical references and index.
Identifiers: LCCN 2024057598 (print) | LCCN 2024057599 (ebook) |
ISBN 9781032349091 (hardback) | ISBN 9781032349107 (paperback) |
ISBN 9781003324409 (ebook)
Subjects: LCSH: Urban density. | Cities and towns—Growth. | City planning.
Classification: LCC HT371 .L43 2025 (print) | LCC HT371 (ebook) |
DDC 307.1/216—dc23/eng/20250331
LC record available at https://lccn.loc.gov/2024057598
LC ebook record available at https://lccn.loc.gov/2024057599

ISBN: 9781032349091 (hbk)
ISBN: 9781032349107 (pbk)
ISBN: 9781003324409 (ebk)

DOI: 10.4324/9781003324409

Typeset in Calibri
by codeMantra

To Arjun and Tejas

To Luc Anselin

Contents

1

INTRODUCTION

Density has always been the measure of cities. The earliest known human settlements identified as *cities, which* appeared in Mesopotamia and the Indus Valley Civilization, were characterized as such on the basis of their high-building density and large, dense populations. Numerous definitions of cities regularly use "density" as the defining concept. According to Wirth (1938), "a city is a relatively large, dense, and permanent settlement of socially heterogenous individuals." Cities are "points of maximum concentration for the power and culture of a community," and "places where a certain energized crowding of people takes place" (Mumford, 1937; Kostof, 1991).

Despite this central importance, density is a relative term with no particular thresholds. Definitions and measurement strategies are numerous, ranging from population or housing units per area (Childe, 1950), to calculations based on an urban systems' social, economic, political, and ecological functions. Further, density is highly context-dependent. Dense apartment buildings in a cornfield are an entirely different concept than density in lower Manhattan. The fundamental and contextual variation in the characteristics associated with urban density—its definition, measurement, context, and evaluation—make the concept difficult to grasp.

Density is also full of paradoxes. One is that cities can be both dispersing and densifying at the same time. For example, one study showed that the densification of the urban core often coincides with substantial suburbanization on the periphery (Tikoudis et al., 2022). Another is that densification can occur outside of city centers, making it difficult to assess whether a city is densifying or not. A study of density patterns in eight Indian cities found that in half the cities the increase in density was largely in peripheral areas, and hence cities were perceived as dispersing rather than densifying (Kotharkar & Bahadure, 2020). A third paradox is that change in density over time follows inconsistent and unexpected patterns. For example, urban economics would predict that population density gradients should become flatter over time—but this is not always the case. Researchers in the Netherlands found the opposite to be true, where Dutch cities had population density gradients that grew steeper between 2000 and 2017 (Broitman & Koomen, 2020).

This complexity and obfuscation are ultimately counterproductive in terms of sustainability goals, since density is exactly what cities need right now. This is especially a problem in the U.S., where cities continue to sprawl, transit-served areas are losing population, and efforts to increase

DOI: 10.4324/9781003324409-1

density are highly contested. There is now a broad consensus that to be sustainable, cities need to be compact, which means they need to have density. They need to be dense in order to maximize access, minimize habitat loss, and promote social connection. They need to be dense to make public transit feasible and more frequent, thereby helping to reduce car traffic. They need to be dense because there is safety in numbers, and density provides more "eyes on the street."

We know these benefits to be true, and yet building compactly—adding density where it's needed—is regularly under attack and/or legally prevented. Much has been written about this problem, but it is our contention that more can be done to better understand how density can be seen in a more positive light. How do we tackle the central problem of density acceptance?

We believe that much of the problem boils down to context. People, we believe, are more likely to view density positively when density is designed well, built in the appropriate place, and contextually synergistic. This also means that while density comes in many forms, in order for density to be seen in a positive light, the devil is in the details. Some forms of density are beneficial and delightful, other forms are not. Some contexts are better for density, others are not. The aim of this book is to flesh out these contextual nuances and present clear and actionable strategies for living closer.

Changing views on density

People started to view density as a significant social and environmental problem sometime in the 19th century—coincident with the rise of industrialized urbanization. Cities struggled with deteriorating housing conditions such as densely packed housing units, substandard hygiene, and poverty that were often associated with destructive fires, disease, and social disorder.

The assumption was that urban density and overcrowding were interchangeable terms. The result was that both planning theory and practice rejected the idea that urban density had value. Jane Jacobs was especially critical of this attitude, stating that the development of modern city planning "has been emotionally based on a glum reluctance to accept city concentrations of people as desirable, and this negative emotion about city concentrations of people has helped deaden planning intellectually" (1961, p. 288).

Even now, when we know that density is an essential part of what it means to build cities sustainably, density is regularly (and erroneously) linked to social and environmental problems such as overcrowding, crime, disease, and pollution (Talen & Wileden, 2024). In the U.S., planning efforts to reduce urban density and protect low-density living are embedded in a whole network of regulatory and policy tools and decisions. There are at least five.[1]

1. *Public health and safety:* In the past it was believed that excessively dense urban conditions directly compromised public health and

safety. Overcrowded residential units around industrial facilities were considered a major threat to public health and safety due to higher risks of fire, pollution, and contagious disease transmissions (Bartlett, 2017). Starting in the early 20th century, the argument was taken up by urban planners and theorists who supported zoning regulations that would reduce urban density. Widely accepted thought maintained that zoning could effectively reduce density by regulating large-scale industrial facilities and thereby protect residential areas and improve their living environment.

2. *Commute choices:* Zoning regulations also separated *home* from *work*, contributing to the suburban sprawl development pattern that overtook the U.S. urban periphery during the post-World War II era. Suburban residential areas and urban cores were connected by highway systems supported by federal highway programs such as the Interstate Highway Act. Added to this was the growth in car ownership—and car affordability—and the result was that many individuals chose *longer* daily commutes to work in pursuit of less density and what was considered a safer and healthier suburban lifestyle.

3. *Housing affordability:* While zoning and government-supported highway construction programs promoted suburban sprawl, other government housing programs such as those administered by the Federal Housing Administration (FHA) and Veterans Administration (VA) loan programs augmented the spread of new single-family housing subdivisions. The FHA and VA programs provided mortgages for more than 11 million new single-family houses located in suburban sprawl neighborhoods. Unfortunately, these programs did not support denser forms of housing construction, such as row houses, townhomes, and residential units combined with mixed-use; resulting in an increase of low-density housing subdivisions. Through a range of government subsidies, these programs made suburban housing appear more affordable. Tax breaks for mortgages translated to a monthly mortgage payment that was often less than a monthly rent.

4. *Property owner preference:* Private property owners in suburban areas were often motivated by a desire for low density, and planning organizations supported these desires via zoning. Accompanying public health and safety concerns, zoning regulations offered private property protection from what was considered "undesirable" land use development in nearby parcels. A growing perception among single-family homeowners was that zoning was a tool that would protect them from detrimental land use and maintain a low-density community. Residential environments perceived as separate and less dense were considered by property owners to be the best protection of their investment. Zoning for low-density stabilized and increased property values.

5. *Environmental aspect:* The belief that excessive urban density compromises public health and safety led to an increased demand for single-family homes with outdoor space close to "nature." With their imposed minimum lot and housing unit sizes, zoning regulations were used to install large residential subdivisions that offered relatively large parcel sizes and often substantial lawn areas. The result was a lower built form of density. This development pattern often included

manipulated natural elements such as lawns and landscaping features, with little consideration of environmental consequences.

These were the mindsets underlying the previous century's push for low density—but the concept of density has drastically changed. As Tonkiss (2014, p. 37) asserted: "the inversion of the language of density is striking: from a social and environmental evil to a positive social and environmental good." Now, the concept of density is embedded in a contemporary urban planning ethos that advocates a *Compact City*. New Urbanism, for example, a prominent urban design movement, promotes "appropriate building densities" that encourage the utilization of public transportation as a viable alternative to automobiles (Steuteville & Langdon, 2009). Highly dense, mixed development located close to transit stations is a key concept of transit-oriented development (TOD), which is also widely promoted. Increased residential density is one of the most important Smart Growth strategies promoted by the Urban Land Institute (Urban Land Institute, 1998) and the American Planning Association (Downs, 2005).

The irony is that these planning efforts advocating urban density in the 21st century are justified based on the same set of planning arguments that rejected urban density in the 20th century.

1. *Public health and safety:* The concept of urban density is one of the determinants of built-environment characteristics that provide mixed land use and pedestrian-friendly residential environments. Public health and safety arguments are based on these density characteristics: proximity to healthy and safer lifestyle opportunities (e.g., parks and green spaces) and easy walkable access to everyday services and facilities (e.g., grocery stores, daycare). Studies have found that living in disadvantaged neighborhoods with inadequate mixed land use and walkable environments are positively associated with lower levels of physical activity and a higher body mass index (BMI) (Doyle et al., 2006; Rundle et al., 2007; Wilson et al., 2008). Relatively dense urban environments that promote a high level of walkability and physical activity have been strongly associated with crime reduction (Foster & Giles-Corti, 2008); such environments promote informal surveillance by "eyes on the street"—natural proprietors of the street such as pedestrians, residents, and retailers (Jacobs, 1961).
2. *Commute choices:* Contemporary planning efforts designed to increase urban density have a strong relationship with preferred daily commute modes, especially public transportation. Public transportation development is highly dependent on various types of density, such as population, job opportunities, and residential and commercial units; greater density insures sufficient and sustainable ridership and enables public transit systems to be economically viable (Guerra et al., 2012). Urban densities that accommodate mixed land uses are linked to commuting options that involve physically active modes (e.g., walking and biking) as well as shorter and safer commutes in all modes.
3. *Housing affordability*: Restrictions on density, especially via exclusionary zoning, lead to higher housing prices (Glaeser, 2012). Higher

residential density, on the other hand, can help mitigate the problem of housing affordability by increasing supply. Such density provides for a greater number of housing units per parcel, and lower land acquisition and construction costs per housing unit. Planning initiatives that support neighborhood density such as form-based codes (FBCs) and Missing Middle Housing (MMH), have emphasized the role of built-form density in affordable housing development. The focus is on promoting housing type diversity and residential-involved mixed-use development, offering various types of affordable housing units.

4. *Property owner preference:* Planning efforts to build urban density are linked to the increasing demand for compact, mixed-use, and walkable neighborhoods. According to the National Association of Realtors Community and Transportation preferences survey (2017, 2020, 2023), walkable access to amenities is an important attribute for Americans of all ages, especially those of the younger Millennials and Gen Z generations who prefer to live in denser and more walkable communities. Similarly, an increased interest in walkable communities is a recent trend among Americans older than 55 and those with higher incomes. This trend has resulted in the promotion and creation of "vibrant, mixed-use neighborhoods with well-connected streets and more compact development" (Schilling & Linton, 2005, p. 96). Recent research also supports this community preference trend by acknowledging the physical, social, and health benefits of living in a walkable neighborhood (Sarkar et al., 2014).

5. *Environmental aspect:* The concept of urban density has impacted urban planning practices related to reducing land consumption and habitat loss, which are frequently associated with mixed land use and infill development. Urban density creates a mix of residential, commercial, and institutional land uses which have the potential to minimize environmental harm (McDonald et al., 2023). High densities encourage sustainable commute modes such as walking, biking, and train and bus usage—which, in turn, reduces transport energy consumption and the carbon footprint. Frequently measured by population count and job opportunities, urban density is a key indicator of automobile ownership associated with sustainability parameters (Sinha, 2003). In the long term, higher density urban development can impact agricultural land retention, biodiversity conservation, and climate change prevention.

Density valuation

The five arguments discussed above affirm that the contextual characteristics of urban density have changed significantly. Initially, urban density was a great concern for urban planning scholars and practitioners, beginning in the century of rapid industrialization (19th) and extending well into the 20th century. Urban density was conceived as being linked to a range of social and environmental problems, especially crime, poverty, and disease.

But urban density discourse in the 21st century is quite different. Urban density now impacts transit modes, reduces commute times, supports lower carbon emission agendas, improves quality of life, and accommodates affordable housing options (Frank & Pivo, 1994; Bardhan et al., 2015; Stein, 2014; Glaeser & Kahn, 2010).

As urban density now plays a crucial role in pursuing economic, environmental, and social improvements, planning researchers and practitioners naturally pay particular attention to the metrics and measures that help operationalize and quantify it. These tend to involve numeric attributes such as land-use restrictions, floor area ratios, minimum lot/house size requirements, and housing unit limits (Burton, 2002; Chen et al., 2020; Berghauser et al., 2021). Planners approach density via regulation, and regulation, in turn, relies on numeric density measures that manipulate the morphological characteristics of the built environment.

Going forward, however, it will be critically important to ensure that urban density is evaluated not as a singular dimension but as a complex concept whose valuation relies on its context. High-density residential developments are incapable of achieving economic, environmental, and social success if residential unit density is merely regulated within a single-use parcel located beyond reasonable proximities to work, services, and facilities. Despite its high-form density, this type of "functional sprawl" is not able to mitigate the problems associated with low-density "spatial sprawl" such as automobile dependency, lack of social diversity, and housing affordability (Tonkiss, 2014, p. 43).

Our book goes beyond conventional density assessment methods and seeks to understand the critical importance of context. We look at the various means of understanding the concept of density by focusing on its contextual characteristics, both structural and functional. Our book fills a gap in the urban density literature by answering the followings questions: (1) How do we contextualize multiple dimensions of urban density based on a structural understanding of it? (2) What are the various forces that influence urban density? (3) How does urban density impact and respond to economic, environmental, and social characteristics? And (4), What are impactful urban design and planning strategies capable of promoting forms of urban density that people will accept, and even prefer?

This book is an attempt to systematically explore the social context of urban density, and how it plays a role in urban design and planning strategies. We take a descriptive approach toward urban density to demonstrate how it can be contextualized, rather than a prescriptive approach in which density is reduced to a numeric regulation. Major challenges are involved along the way, both in capturing the built environment's complexity, and in deciding what factors are needed to better understand urban density physically as well as socially. We believe that cities and places have unique cultures and identities, and a wide range of considerations need to be taken into account in the attempt to insert more density. This book acknowledges this relationship—between urban density and social and physical context—and investigates the ways in which density can use this context to enhance livability and promote a more sustainable world.

Note

1   The discussion about changing views on density was inspired by Sonia Hirt's discussion on historic arguments for mixed use. Hirt, S. A. (2016). Rooting out mixed use: Revisiting the original rationales. *Land Use Policy, 50*, 134–147.

Literature cited

Bardhan, R., Kurisu, K., & Hanaki, K. (2015). Does compact urban forms relate to good quality of life in high density cities of India? Case of Kolkata. *Cities, 48*, 55–65.

Bartlett, K. (2017). *The health of nations: The campaign to end polio and eradicate epidemic diseases*. London: Simon and Schuster.

Berghauser Pont, M., & Haupt, P. (2021). *Spacematrix: Space, density and urban form* Rotterdam, the Netherlands: Naio10 Publishers.

Broitman, D., & Koomen, E. (2020). The attraction of urban cores: Densification in Dutch city centres. *Urban Studies, 57*(9), 1920–1939. https://doi.org/10.1177/0042098019864019

Burton, E. (2002). Measuring urban compactness in UK towns and cities. *Environment and planning B: Planning and Design, 29*(2), 219–250.

Chen, H. Y., Chowdhury, R., McFarlane, C., & Tripathy, P. (2020). Introduction: Rethinking urban density. *Urban Geography, 41*(10), 1241–1246.

Childe, V. G. (1950). The urban revolution. *Town Planning Review, 21*(1), 3.

Downs, A. (2005). Smart growth: Why we discuss it more than we do it. *Journal of the American Planning Association, 71*(4), 367–378.

Doyle, S., Kelly-Schwartz, A., Schlossberg, M., & Stockard, J. (2006). Active community environments and health: The relationship of walkable and safe communities to individual health. *Journal of the American Planning Association, 72*(1), 19–31.

Foster, S., & Giles-Corti, B. (2008). The built environment, neighborhood crime and constrained physical activity: An exploration of inconsistent findings. *Preventive Medicine, 47*(3), 241–251.

Frank, L. D., & Pivo, G. (1994). Impacts of mixed use and density on utilization of three modes of travel: Single-occupant vehicle, transit, and walking. *Transportation Research Record, 1466*, 44–52.

Glaeser, E. (2012). *Triumph of the city: How our greatest invention makes us richer, smarter, greener, healthier, and happier*. New York: Penguin Books.

Glaeser, E. L., & Kahn, M. E. (2010). The greenness of cities: Carbon dioxide emissions and urban development. *Journal of Urban Economics, 67*(3), 404–418.

Guerra, E., Cervero, R., & Tischler, D. (2012). Half-mile circle: Does it best represent transit station catchments? *Transportation Research Record, 2276*(1), 101–109.

Jacobs, J. (1961). *The death and life of great American cities*. New York, NY: Vintage Books.

Kostof, S. (1991). *The city shaped: Urban patterns and meanings through history*. Boston, MA: Little, Brown and Co.

Kotharkar, R., & Bahadure, P. (2020). Achieving compact city form through density distribution: Case of Indian cities. *Journal of Urban Planning and Development, 146*(1), 04019022. https://doi.org/10.1061/(ASCE)UP.1943-5444.0000529.

McDonald, R. I., Aronson, M. F., Beatley, T., Beller, E., Bazo, M., Grossinger, R., …, & Spotswood, E. (2023). Denser and greener cities: Green interventions to achieve both urban density and nature. *People and Nature, 5*(1), 84–102. https://doi.org/10.1002/pan3.10423.

Mumford, L. (1937). What is a city? *Architectural Record, 82*(5), 59–62.

National Association of Realtors (2017). *The 2173 national community and transportation preferences survey.* Washington, DC: American Strategies and Myers Research, Strategic Services, LLC.

National Association of Realtors (2020). *The 2020 national community and transportation preferences survey.* Washington, DC: American Strategies and Myers Research, Strategic Services, LLC.

National Association of Realtors (2023). *The 2023 national community and transportation preferences survey.* Washington, DC: American Strategies and Myers Research, Strategic Services, LLC.

Rundle, A., Roux, A. V. D., Freeman, L. M., Miller, D., Neckerman, K. M., & Weiss, C. C. (2007). The urban built environment and obesity in New York City: A multilevel analysis. *American Journal of Health Promotion*, 21(4_suppl), 326–334. https://doi.org/10.4278/0890-1171-21.4s.326.

Sarkar, C., Webster, C., & Gallacher, J. (2014). *Healthy cities: Public health through urban planning.* Edward Elgar Publishing. https://www.elgaronline.com/monobook/9781781955710.xml.

Schilling, J., & Linton, L. S. (2005). The public health roots of zoning: In search of active living's legal genealogy. *American Journal of Preventive Medicine*, 28(2), 96–104.

Sinha, K. C. (2003). Sustainability and urban public transportation. *Journal of Transportation Engineering*, 129(4), 331–341.

Stein, S. (2014). De Blasio's doomed housing plan. *Jacobin Magazine.* Available at: https://jacobin.com/2014/10/de-blasios-doomed-housing-plan/ (accessed August 2024).

Steuteville, R., & Langdon, P. (2009). *New urbanism: Best practices guide* (4th ed., expanded and completely rev.). Ithaca, NY: New Urban News Publications.

Talen, E., & Wileden, L. (2024). The density puzzle: What is known, what is disputed, and where to go from here. *Journal of Planning Literature*, 08854122241262750.

Tikoudis, I., Farrow, K., Mebiame, R. M., & Oueslati, W. (2022). Beyond average population density: Measuring sprawl with density-allocation indicators. *Land Use Policy*, 112, 105832. https://doi.org/10.1016/j.landusepol.2021.105832.

Tonkiss, F. (2014). *Cities by design: The social life of urban form.* Hoboken, NJ: John Wiley & Sons.

Urban Land Institute. (1998). *Smart growth: Economy, community, environment.* Washington, DC: Urban Land Institute.

Wilson, S., Hutson, M., & Mujahid, M. (2008). How planning and zoning contribute to inequitable development, neighborhood health, and environmental injustice. *Environmental Justice*, 1(4), 211–216. https://doi.org/10.1089/env.2008.0506.

Wirth, L. (1938). Urbanism as a way of life. *American Journal of Sociology*, 44(1), 1–24.

2

DENSITY IN THREE CONTEXTS: AN INTERPRETATION

Housing in a park, Part I: Towers to townhouses

In the first kind of context, housing from high-rise towers to low-rise apartment buildings and townhomes is set in open space. The category includes the famous (or infamous) "towers in a park" model. Often, large parcels are used to promote containment and insularity, and buildings are treated as isolated objects in space rather than as part of a larger interconnected urban fabric. Buildings are set in green space in a quest to make them more "natural." Or the housing itself might be curved to make it look natural, such as the Hilliard Tower Apartments in Chicago, a public housing project (shown in Figure 2.1). Streets might be replaced with parks, although doing so usually results in more separation and more cars, and more cars needed to be put somewhere, like parking lots.

The modernist architect Le Corbusier (1964 [1937]) was convinced that high-rise living and towers in parks created the utmost in individual liberty because, guided by the laws of geometry and technological perfection, it freed people from "ignorance and conflict." High-rises were monuments to rationality and the "rule of reason."

There has been a lot of critique of the arrangement. Jane Jacobs (1961) interpreted housing towers set in green space as a celebration of "the potency of statistics and the triumph of the mathematical average."

 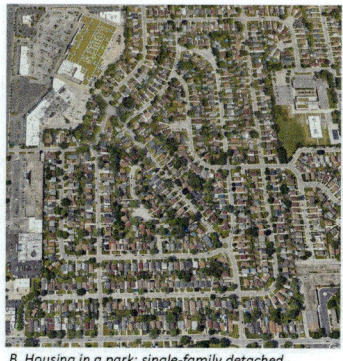 

A. Housing in a park: towers
Gross density: 13.2 units per acre

B. Housing in a park: single-family detached
Gross density: 4.2 units per acre

C. Old urbanism
Gross density: 22.3 units per acre

Figure 2.1 Example densities in three contexts.

DOI: 10.4324/9781003324409-2

The high-rise symbolized machine living, the monotony and regimentation of human life by invisible corporate forces, the rule of bureaucracy. Since they separate people from the ground and therefore their surroundings, it is hard to read them as liberators. High-rise living is regularly interpreted as a place of alienation—from other people and from the outside world (Mumford, 1962; Braunfels, 1990). Social mingling does not come easily: one must have a dedicated reason to venture out and socialize.

But towers in parks can be viewed as a reconciliation of density and green space, where the ground has been "freed" for greenery. There is certainly a bold symbolism expressed in a skyscraper set in green space. One is seclusion—or isolation. Each building is an island or, if lined up in successive rows as they sometimes were, dominoes. Parkchester in New York was an early cluster of towers in a park, built in the 1940s. High-rises set in parks were not garden city decentralization, but there was a certain relationship between the two concepts, as both involved trying to get nearer to greenspace.

The problem with the isolation of buildings was, as Oscar Newman (1972) and others pointed out, that it resulted in a disregard for the functional use of the spaces surrounding buildings. It was the superblock, the loosening up of traditional urban streets and blocks, that made the public realm ambiguous and indecipherable. Stuyvesant Town-Peter Cooper Village in New York City, shown in Figure 2.2, is a good example. The development has 11,200 residents on their own two superblocks, closed off by surrounding arterials, inwardly focused on their own green space, and definitely not a part of the Manhattan grid. In this way, proponents argued, Stuyvesant Town created a peaceful district that was a welcomed contrast to the rigidity and chaos of Manhattan.

But in public housing environments, there seemed to be no appreciation for the fact that there is a crucial difference between visual open space and habitable open space. Because of the failure to appreciate the importance of context and the need to create connectedness between buildings, buildings became ensconced in vast expanses of asphalt, useless plazas, and other forms of what Trancik labeled "lost space" (Trancik, 1986). There was no possibility of natural forms of surveillance and "eyes on the street."

Figure 2.2 Stuyvesant Town—Peter Cooper Village, Manhattan, New York.

A defining feature of this kind of density is that housing is set in a superblock—not the Barcelona kind of superblock in which city blocks are combined and closed to traffic to create pedestrianized public space, and where circulation and movement are no longer dominated by the automobile but are instead a mix of walking, biking, transit. Rather, the superblock that accommodates towers and apartment buildings consists of blocks in which the buildings within them are unaligned with streets. Buildings are set in open land, untethered. There is no street frontage, per se. Streets are thus not the primary organizing element of urban form, and as a result their significance is seriously downgraded. The obvious liability of the superblock is that it cuts off access. Even if traversed with pedestrian pathways, the paths are not lined with activities. If there is no meaningful destination at either end, and no variation in the scenes one can experience along the way, the pathways can become somewhat meaningless.

Proponents of this arrangement loved the opening up of the city to "nature," giving apartment dwellers immediate access to green space. High-rise slabs could be oriented for sun exposure on two sides for every unit, thanks to superblock freedom. It would also free people from the dense grid that was thought to constrain freedom. The reasoning was that buildings with low land coverage and exposure to open space outweighed any social connectivity benefit that a grid with small blocks might provide. This was not thought to result in less social connectivity. The superblock allowed buildings to relate to each other rather than to the street, which advocates believed would improve social connection.

Apart from access to green space and the impression of freedom, it was not lost on city leaders that superblocks could save money: fewer streets means lower land cost. The use of large blocks to lessen the need for street-building was a motivation behind Berlin's much criticized apartment blocks, although there it was not a matter of apartments set in green space. But even where the objective of the superblock was to increase access to greenspace, reducing road-building cost was still a strong motive.

In the U.S. case, the superblocks that housed towers or apartment buildings incorporated a curvilinear street design, although an interesting evolutionary step toward the superblock was the case of apartment buildings set in gridded green space, such as Jackson Heights in Queens, New York. The design was novel at the time—a community composed of six-story apartment buildings set in a grid with plenty of green. From there, the next step toward modernist superblock form was to eliminate all but the outermost streets and embrace the freedom to locate buildings randomly within the created park.

Radburn, New Jersey, built in 1929, is the quintessential superblock community and the place where the separation of traffic was introduced into the American consciousness. Attached houses front green spaces rather than streets, and the green area defines neighborhood boundaries. Neighborhoods were thus conceived as grouped housing around a central open space, and the "community heart and backbone" was a park. Superblocks were also useful for accomplishing complete separation of pedestrian and car. Other developments followed Radburn's example. Baldwin Hills Village in Los Angeles, shown in Figure 2.3, now called the "Village Green," was a superblock champion (Stein, 1951).

Jane Jacobs didn't like this lower density version of housing set in parks, either. She denounced these surrounded interior greens, which she called "sheltered 'togetherness' worlds." She argued that they were exclusively matriarchal and really only of use to very small children— which means they are yet another form of specialization and separation. With buildings turning their back on the street, superblocks emblemized the travesty that private cars have been given the authority to dictate the urban pattern.

The modernist, low-rise apartment building set in open space is known as "dense sprawl." In some ways, it is the worst of all worlds: density without amenities, and without usable open space. The "townhouses" of sprawl are apartments without towns. People living in them are forced to live densely without any of the usual compensations. At least towers in parks are likely to house a lot more people and therefore support more services.

Similar to "towers in a park", low-rise apartments in a park erased historical building tradition, usually employing a boxy, stripped down kind of architecture with an institutional quality. A good example is Aluminum City Terrace near Pittsburgh (Figure 2.4). But in addition to a desire to

Figure 2.3 Baldwin Hills, Los Angeles, California.

Figure 2.4 Aluminum City Terrace near Pittsburgh, Pennsylvania.

separate from history there was also separation from the surrounding city, which was accomplished by a street pattern that minimized street connection. Perhaps there would be only one or two street intersections, which created an unfortunate aggregation of traffic at these junctures. Links to the exterior street system were kept to an absolute minimum.

Also impactful was a formulaic attachment to the principles of maximizing exposure to sun and greenspace. Houses fronted green space rather than streets, and the orientation was north-south to maximize sunlight in every room. In similar, single-purpose fashion, the attached housing of Aluminum City Terrace near Pittsburgh reveals that the only real consideration was solar orientation. The superblock created the ability of buildings to be arranged for maximizing sun exposure, and this was interpreted as promoting spatial equity.

Sun exposure, worked out mathematically to dictate the space between buildings, was prioritized at the expense of any social priorities, like the creation of enclosed space or the recognition of streets as a setting for social encounter. To eliminate shadows, buildings could be set at right angles to the street, perpendicular and never facing them. Social exchange via the street was eliminated since there was to be no traffic—and thus no street—between buildings. Streets were treated like service lanes. And yet, the ability of green space to foster social connection can be difficult since green space is a passive social space, not a space in which social interaction naturally springs from people engaged in daily tasks. In contrast, traditional city form with its spatial definition, continuous building frontage, integrated elements, mixed uses, and unambiguous spaces enabled social encounter in an unprogrammed and organic way: spontaneous social interaction was woven into the flows of everyday social exchange.

Clusters of apartment blocks usually translated to no private outdoor space, no strict separation of public and private. Building placement was mechanistic and might be called "crane urbanism" as the site layout was related to the maximum reach of a crane machine. When housing is rationalized and machine-based, it reads like a cold calculation intended to manipulate, control, and sometimes even incarcerate (often poor) people.

Housing in a park, Part II: Single-family suburbs

The low-density suburb is defined by segregated uses, car dependence, and a rejection of the street with its aligned frontages and spatial definition. Housing is separated, the automobile is prioritized over the pedestrian, and the street is not regarded as a public space. In this it has much in common with any other kind of housing set in green space, including towers. The historic version of it is the planned suburb or the garden suburb. The modern version is known as sprawl.

Admittedly, historic versions of separated houses in suburban contexts are quite different from sprawl, although the density is similar. The former consists of railroad suburbs or garden suburbs, and usually started with a strong node such as a train station, around which the suburb developed. In sprawl, formulating such a congealing node would be incongruous, since the point of sprawl is the individual realization of one's own version of suburban life, where one is free to drive here and there to piece that realization together. Unlike sprawl with its libertarian bent, the planned suburb tried to instill communal principles in its design. At Bedford Park, for example, separate houses and separate gardens were thought to stimulate "a more responsive citizenship" (Creese, 1992).

This is why some argue that the suburbs that emerged in the 19th century around major cities in the U.S. and Great Britain were a very different kind of lived experience—and although similar in density, different from American low-density sprawl. If there was an attached retail area, as in the planned garden suburb, proponents saw them as a happy combination of "the intensity of the inner-city and the passivity of nature" (Stern et al., 2013).

But others find it difficult to appreciate the green, leafy suburb in any version. Spiro Kostof (1991), labeled garden suburbs as simply "housing schemes" involving "a suburban grid with some curves." Early on, they were distained as quests for a sedentary, un-aspirational life. One commentator wrote of the "homogenous civilization" being created in the suburb; another wrote that the suburbs were sterile and neutral, "haemaphrodite beastliness" arising from a "pitiful attitude of escape" (Sharp, 1936; Masterman, 1909). Jane Jacobs read them as an attempt to block future growth and freeze life in place.

Through the suburb, the bourgeois elite realized their goal "to enjoy all the advantages of the massive urban economy while escaping its perils" (Fishman, 1987), and thus the planned suburb is paradoxical, as Fishman observed, in that it is the product of "two opposing forces ... attraction and repulsion." It is both "an explosive urban expansion and a desperate protest against it." Thus the bourgeois elite created the urban industrial world, but used the planned suburb to escape it. And there is another embedded paradox: the expanding suburban periphery of the middle class helped create an urban core that, as the concentrated center of capital accumulation and wealth generation, became increasingly unaffordable.

Single-family detached housing is the manifestation of separation from one's neighbors. The need to ensure that residents were experiencing a pastoral life meant that social separation was required. To carry the illusion, each house at Riverside, IL (Figure 2.5), the iconic garden suburb west of Chicago laid out by Frederick Law Olmsted in 1869, was required to be setback 30 ft from the sidewalk. Single-family separated houses denote individualism and an inward focus. One irony, though, was that such housing, at least in a peripheral suburban context, can not be understood on its own, but always "in relation to its rejected opposite: the metropolis." What was being rejected was a city increasingly populated with Catholics and Jews. And it represented something more vulnerable: insecurity about the "fragility" of the economic system it relied on. The planned suburb was a monument built not to express faith and assurance, but to construct the "appearance" of confidence. The "dual legacy" of the planned suburb is, on the one hand, the beauty that suburban design could be, but on the other, a physical expression of "bourgeois anxieties" and hatred for the "others" inhabiting the city.

Figure 2.5 Riverside, Illinois.

Most early suburbs like Riverside were meant for the affluent—or as Olmsted put it, "the more intelligent and more fortunate classes," although housing for domestic servants was provided near the railroad tracks. It was the quintessential "bourgeois utopia," to use Robert Fishman's phrase, "a collective assertion of class wealth and privilege as impressive as any medieval castle." Olmsted insisted that Riverside was an integral part of the city by virtue of the rail connecting city and suburb.

The green, leafy, separated housing experience was another aspect of exclusion: cutting out the grayness of cities, with their concrete and noise. A ruralized aesthetic, it was hoped, would better connect people to "nature" and to "the land." This inspired certain design regularities: lots of green lawns, deep setbacks, and low building height—which allows inhabitants to be even closer to the ground, that is, nature. It implied a quest for leisure and freedom from toil, which is ironic given that historically, living in the countryside meant one had to work the land for a living (Kreiger, 2019).

The single-family housing suburb constitutes the selling of "a triple dream, house plus nature plus community" (Hayden, 2003). Each family maintains their own piece of the park, and thus fulfills a civic duty. In Riverside, small green islands are sprinkled throughout the plan, the residuals of the intersections of oddly shaped blocks. And while there are plenty of public areas (constituting one-third of Riverside's total area), but it is the generous front lawns—too public to be part of private family life—that provide the impression of a singular community united in a natural setting (Schuyler, 2019). Still, there are versions, like Riverside, where houses are grouped and positioned in a way that acknowledges and respects collective life, and perhaps even social interaction needs. There is a search for balance. Raymond Unwin's metric was that the planned suburb should have 12 houses to the acre, since more would be "overcrowding," but fewer would not provide the necessary sense of community (Unwin, 1909).

In pursuit of the imitation of nature, suburbs rejected urban forms more conducive to a unified design, like attached row housing and squares, and relied instead on separated family homes embedded in nature. Villas might be clustered around some kind of green central common, but if houses around it were too clustered (and thus urban-ish), the illusion was somewhat harder to maintain. More likely than a central commons was the front lawn—not really private family space, but collectively, at least, an institution. Park settings, nature, rural life, the picturesque—applied to the suburb, these descriptive qualities signal an infusion of nature. Of note, of course, is that the greenwashing is decidedly not a more sustainable, "green" approach to human settlement.

A slightly higher density version of detached housing arrived immediately after World War II in places like Levittown, NY (Figure 2.6), where identical houses on identical lots happened on a vast scale. This signaled production building like never before: housing as commodity that could be cheaply constructed and easily bought and sold. On the plus side, it was a method able to satisfy "the acquisitive urge" of a booming middle class. After World War II, housing production was transformed into an industry, with standardized parts, labor, and processes.

But the uniformity associated with mass scale housing production can be bleak. In Levittown, concern for community spaces and artful groupings of humanly scaled apartments buildings (which occurred in planned suburbs like Radburn) was all but forgotten in favor of churning out single-family houses at record speed. Over time, variety was introduced in incremental ways: small additions, bespoke landscaping, diverse house colors. But the uniform density of Levittown seemed like the physical manifestation of William H. Whyte's (1956) "Org Man"—someone whose life and thoughts are controlled by the "organization" rather than by any personal thoughts or drives.

The worst case of single-family housing in a park is aptly called sprawl, an amorphous blob of housing and related development spreading out over the landscape. There is often great curvilinearity, which in the context of sprawl usually translates to wastefulness—meandering, indirect routes that increase asphalt coverage for no practical reason. The composition is of housing pods rather than neighborhoods. With low densities, excessive open space, and separated buildings, defining neighborhoods in more traditional ways, such as through a neighborhoods center or a defined public realm, is unlikely. But sprawl is not unintentional—houses

Figure 2.6 Levittown, New York.

are arranged and separated according to zoning rules and subdivision ordinances requiring wide separation. Planned sprawl is a strange paradox, and critics have mused about how sprawl can look so disordered when the objective is solely about profit (Gottdeiner, 1977).

Most often, development is organized around freeways and widely spaced arterials, not a defining node capable of providing meaning and wholeness to the surrounding housing. Except for the shopping malls, which are detached and car-dependent, the residential areas of sprawl lack integrated amenities or services. There is a sense of survivalism in this dispersion. Victor Gruen, the shopping mall champion, argued that there was a need to spread the population out to make it "less vulnerable to bombing attacks," and he was happy to meet the commercial needs of sprawl by consolidating shopping in the form of malls (Mennel, 2004).

Robert Fishman (1987) argues that modern, post-1945 sprawl is fundamentally different from the planned suburb because with sprawl the home-work separation ceased to be a motivating factor. Office parks and housing are combined into "an ugly and wasteful pseudo-city, too spread out to be efficient, too superficial to create a true culture," but its detachment from the central city is "profoundly antiurban as suburbia never had been."

Low-density sprawl is universalized for the masses, enabled by the car, subsidized by freeways, and driven solely by profit-making. It shows a highly developed ability to cut corners and maximize profit by streamlining the production process. There is an attitude of excess and waste: overly generous lot sizes and redundant road-building. Housing tracts, and the houses within them, are large and eat up the landscape with no sense of constraint. The excess is particularly American (although China is catching up).

Vast expanses of low-density housing at the outskirts of cities reveals the power dynamics at play: the banking, construction, and real estate sectors, kept afloat through government subsidy and tax breaks. Real Estate Investment Trusts (REITs) buy and sell sprawl components on Wall Street, meaning that investors, far removed from the built environments being created, have no real stake in what is happening on the ground.

Like all housing set in parks, a defining feature of sprawl is separation— of buildings, functions, and spaces. This means there are many open spaces. The openness gives sprawl a veneer of adaptability and leeway to make changes. In theory, standing alone, untethered to any neighbors, isolated buildings do seem to engender "freedom." But the irony is that the geographic spread of sprawl is often the opposite of freedom. Instead, the disarray imposes significant burdens because of the increased distances required to access what is needed for daily life. This is probably why Le Corbusier (1929) rejected the single-family house and proclaimed its inhabitants "slaves."

Widely separated housing also reads loudly of escape, especially escape from the urban poor, which is ironic because many suburbs are, increasingly, poor. In the detached and disorienting world of sprawl, residents might think of themselves as absolved from needing to care about the social and economic problems of the city, or the needs of people who rent rather than own their homes. And while it's true that the single-family house on its own lot is a building type meant to be owned, the fact that suburban homes are increasingly rented presents a certain irony.

Escape and exclusion are why many have argued that low-density sprawl has a high-moral cost. Aspirations of social equity are unlikely, as privatism and consumption are valorized. Political culture is also greatly weakened, as low-density housing is more about privacy than citizen engagement, climate change activism, or social equality. Houses set on private lots are an effort to assert seclusion, an escape from collective life. On the other hand, one could argue, as Melvin Webber (1963) did, that the "non-place" urban realm of sprawl is simply an expression of people connecting and communicating technologically. Digital communication might foster the same density of interaction as any physical form of density—maybe even more. Form and content can be separate and independent.

And yet, when mass-produced products are distributed over a large, mass-produced space, it tends to reduce culture to the lowest common denominator. What emerges, Fishman (1987) argues, is "crass conformity," and a "crucial loss of texture." The low-density of sprawl, in other words, translates to a lack of cultural diversity, since there is only enough critical mass to sustain a single culture. Whatever cultural diversity does exist is not something experienced spontaneously, walking down the street. Because of the low density and spread, social contact is easily avoided or tends to be pre-arranged via the car. There is no opportunity for chance encounters or random social interaction. Mumford (1961) argued that this lack of ability to spontaneously interact not only negates the possibility of collective action but produces "silent conformity" in society.

Low-density detached housing is a counter-weight to what some saw as the socialistic tendency of attached housing. U.S. Secretary of Labor William B. Wilson summed up the sentiment in 1919: "the man who owns his own home is the least susceptible to the so-called Bolshevist doctrines and is about the last man to join in the industrial disturbances fomented by the radical agitators" (Sutcliffe, 1981).

Old urbanism

Housing in parks, whether in towers, apartments, or single-family suburbs, can be contrasted with older urban housing in traditional urban neighborhoods—we'll call it "old urbanism." Urban neighborhoods come in many forms, but a typical example in the U.S. case is an older, urban neighborhood with a mix of housing types, including small apartment buildings and small single-family dwellings on narrow lots. They are almost always gridded, which means that housing on the grid is part of a network connecting it to whatever else is on the network. Compared to other street systems, grids are often thought to have the highest level of connectivity. They prioritize connection and access over other goals, like protection, security, or the emulation of nature—the goals of the housing in a park model. Short, gridded blocks are considered better than long ones for pedestrians, simply because pedestrians will have an easier time walking through the city, if blocks are kept small (Frederick & Mehta, 2018). To be fair, the grid has also been blamed for sanctioning oppressive forms of housing, especially in the 19th century as cities sought to house industrial workers. One example is the gridded, uniform street and lot pattern associated with 19th century "bye-law" housing in England, where "unified rows of repetitive design" created dismal conditions. And of course, in many American cities, such as Chicago, the grid became an essential enabler of capitalist greed, where lots could be easily laid out and sold in speculative fashion (Kostof, 1991).

In the U.S., many older urban neighborhoods started, technically, as suburbs. The earliest suburbs were either relatively close to an existing city's downtown, or linked via public transit, giving them a very urban feel (in other words, their origin as separate suburbs is now barely recognizable). Brooklyn Heights is an example. A related category, in terms of the experience of density, is the Streetcar suburb, which occupied what Chicago School sociologists termed "the zone of emergence"—meaning, emergence out of the much less desirable tenement house neighborhoods (Woods & Kennedy, 1962).

These urban suburbs are much higher density than post-World War II suburbs that emerged in the urban periphery. In old urbanism, the size of single-family houses and lots were kept small, which for a time prevented the city from spreading out excessively. And since they were laid out in a pre-automobile era, they tend to have walkable access to services and amenities. They are also often socially diverse, in part because their housing stock tends to have a mix of small apartments, single-family homes, duplexes, and housing over retail shops. Also, because housing is often attached, and because of their incorporation of retail streets, they tend to have a sense of enclosure—aligned building frontage that creates an outdoor room. If the frontage line is relatively straight, with no projecting buildings, it shows housing's deference to the street and sidewalk and an acknowledgment of the street's role in sustaining social life. Connected houses have energy efficiencies, and are also profitable because they make use of every inch of frontage, which can be valuable real estate.

The contrast between these older urban suburbs and more recent suburbs is that the latter are set in green and leafy picturesque settings where buildings are placed within space—they do not create space or enclosure. Continuity in low-density suburbs is by way of linkages between open spaces, a "continuity of voids," as Choay wrote (1969). Value is based on the amount of light, air, and green space available, not on the creation of a public outdoor room. Houses are in their own private domains. The parks and greenspaces they sit in are not so much contributions to public life as they are extensions of private life.

Old urbanism with its varied housing types was not sequestered and separated. Buildings were also often mixed use, such as having housing over stores. The social implications of this were significant. The merchant's house was "open to the city" and families were integrated into "wider networks of urban amusements." Later, as Fishman (1987) analyzed in his seminal work, *Bourgeois Utopias*, a profound division between home and work emerged, between "the feminine/natural/emotional world of the family and the masculine/rational/urban world of work." Unlike old urbanism, outlying suburbs provided a way to manifest these new conceptions of family and the role of women, where city and family were put in contradiction.

There is another way that the aligned frontage of old urbanism presented a very different experience of density. In low-density single-family suburbs, as Frederick and Mehta (2018) note, land is "organized by purpose," the experience is "selective, single-variable, and destination-centric." The experience of urban neighborhoods, on the other hand, is "continuous, oblique, and incidental." In the low-density case, people walk perpendicular, car to door. Each destination has its own purpose. In old urbanism, people walk parallel rather than perpendicular, and destinations are experienced "all-at-once rather than one-at-a-time." The difference has obvious implications for social and economic connectivity and inter-dependence.

Sometimes the neighborhoods of old urbanism were predominantly single-family, but because of their clustering, shared walls, and alignment, that did not mean they were low in density. In the high-density version of old urbanism, characteristic of older urban neighborhoods, the pre-zoning rules of city building created a tight configuration, even of single-family houses. In the oldest cities, lots could be quite narrow, such as the 16-foot lots permitted in Washington, DC (Figure 2.7). Single-family housing was attached. Joseph Stübben (1890), writing in 1890, recognized the many advantages of attached buildings ("building in blocks"). They required less ground, were better suited for business purposes, cost less to build, made heating easier, and were safer because only the

Figure 2.7 Washington, DC.

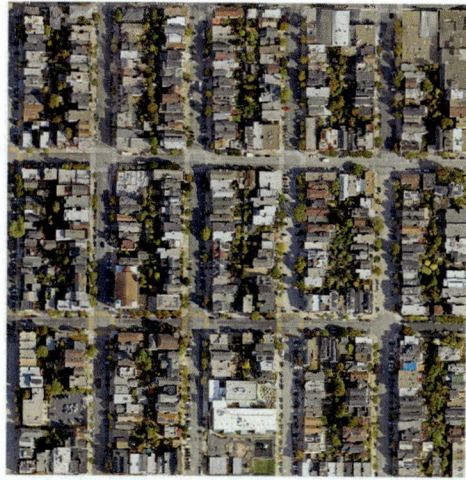

*A. San Francisco, California
25 ft. wide lots, 480 housing units*

*B. Cave Creek, Arizona
75 ft. wide lots, 75 housing units*

Figure 2.8 A quarter-mile square in San Francisco, California and Cave Creek, Arizona.

front of the building was accessible. "It would therefore be folly to make detached building the rule in cities," he wrote.

When zoning took over the city-building process, the context of single-family housing changed radically. In low-density sprawl, the pattern of houses spreading out was a result of rules about maximum units per acre, minimum lot size per unit, minimum street frontage per unit (thus making units behind the main structure infeasible), front yard setbacks that eliminated the possibility of additional units on a lot, sideyards that eliminate the possibility of rowhouses and duplexes, and the requirement that each unit must have a separate driveway. Figure 2.8 shows the differences. Each image shows lots within the same land area: a quarter-mile square. San Francisco, California, has 25 ft wide lots. Cave Creek, Arizona, has 75 ft wide lots. The difference in land use efficiency is enormous. The 25 ft wide lots of San Francisco yield 480 single-family dwellings. The 75 ft wide lots of Cave Creek yield about 70 dwellings.

References

Braunfels, W. (1990). *Urban design in Western Europe: Regime and architecture, 900–1900*. Translated by Kenneth J. Northcott. Chicago, IL: University of Chicago Press.

Choay, F. (1969). *The modern city: Planning in the 19th century*. New York: George Braziller.

Creese, W. L. (1992). *The search for environment*. Baltimore, MD: The Johns Hopkins University Press.

Fishman, R. (1987). *Bourgeois Utopias: The rise and fall of suburbia*. New York: Basic Books.

Frederick, M., & Mehta, V. (2018). *101 Things I learned in urban design school*. New York: Three Rivers Press.

Gottdiener, M. (1977). *Planned sprawl: Private and public interests in suburbia*. Beverly Hills, CA: Sage.

Hayden, D. (2003). *Building suburbia: Green fields and urban growth, 1820–2000*. New York: Pantheon Books.

Jacobs, J. (1961). *The death and life of great American cities*. New York: Vintage Books.

Kostof, S. (1991). *The city shaped*. London: Thames and Hudson.

Kreiger, A. (2019). *City on a hill: Urban idealism in America from the puritans to the present*. Cambridge, MA: Belknap Press.

Le Corbusier. (1929). *The city of tomorrow and its planning*. New York: Dover.

Le Corbusier. (1964 (1937)). *When the Cathedrals were White*. New York: McGraw-Hill.

Masterman, C. F. G. (1909). *The condition of England*. London: Metheun.

Mennel, T. (2004). Victor Gruen and the construction of Cold War Utopias. *Journal of Planning History, 3*(2), 116–150.

Mumford, L. (1961). *The city in history: Its origins, its transformations, and its prospects*. New York: Harcourt Brace Jovanovich.

Mumford, L. (1962, December). Megalopolis as anti-city. *Architectural Record, 132*(6). 101–108.

Newman, O. (1972). *Defensible space: Crime prevention through urban design*. New York: Macmillan.

Schuyler, D. (2019). Riverside: The first comprehensively designed suburban community in the United States. In M. C. Sies, I. Gournay, & R. Freestone, Eds., *Iconic planned communities and the challenge of change* (pp. 40–60). Philadelphia: University of Pennsylvania Press.

Sharp, T. (1936). *English Panorama*. London: Dent.

Stein, C. (1951). *Toward new Towns for America*. Liverpool: University Press of Liverpool.

Stern, R. A. M., Fishman, D., & Tilove, J. (2013). *Planned paradise: The garden suburb and the modern city*. New York: The Monacelli Press.

Stübben, J. (1890). *City building (Der Städtebau)*. Reprint of the 1st ed., Braunschweig Vieweg. https://uchicago.app.box.com/s/nequkaloacwqv8p38 2qc13htvbldmafc.

Sutcliffe, A. (1981). *Towards the planned city: German, Britain, the United States and France 1780–1914*. New York: St. Martin's Press.

Trancik, R. (1986). *Finding lost space*. New York: Van Nostrand Reinhold.

Unwin, R. (1909). *Town planning in practice*. London: T. Fisher Unwin.

Webber, M. M. (1963). Order in diversity: Community without propinquity. In L. Wingo, Ed., *Cities and space: The future use of urban land* (pp. 22–54). Baltimore, MD: Johns Hopkins University Press.

Whyte, W. H. (1956). *Organization man*. New York: Simon and Schuster.

Woods, R. A., & Kennedy, A. J. (1962). *The zone of emergence: Observations of the lower middle and upper working class communities of Boston, 1905–1914*. Cambridge: MIT Press.

3

THE SPATIAL PATTERN OF DENSITY: DOES IT MAKE SENSE?

Spatial density and equity

Density plays a crucial role in achieving various urban planning benefits, such as ensuring greater and fairer access to amenities, services, and facilities. It is believed that density brings the equal distribution of public goods, services, resources, and opportunities, which is linked to the concept of social equity in urban planning. Research in this area has shown evidence of discrimination in the spatial distribution of public services, educational opportunities, and access to a safer and healthier environment (Ratner, 1968; Haar & Fessler, 1986; Been, 1992). Density has been recognized as a powerful tool that has a positive impact on social equity.

The concept of social equity aims to ensure that everyone has fair opportunities and outcomes. According to McKenzie (2004), it involves providing equitable chances for all. Colantonio (2010, p. 84) defines equity as having "access to sufficient resources to participate fully in community life and sufficient opportunities for personal development and advancement." Woodcraft (2012) emphasizes the importance of access to amenities and infrastructure as key components of social sustainability, laying the groundwork for a thriving community.

Fairness in distributing resources and providing equal access to economic resources and services are key principles for building a socially sustainable community (Cuthill, 2010). Some practical examples include ensuring that public transport services are accessible to the elderly, poor, and disabled; providing fair access to affordable housing and job opportunities; and ensuring equal access to community health and education services. Density is part of social equity and justice strategies, as it enables better access to services and opportunities for a wide range of people.

The relationship between spatial density patterns and social equity has been discussed in relation to its positive association with social benefits of accessibility. Density is often associated with mixed land use that provides convenient access to services and facilities within walkable proximity and improves walkability and accessibility. It is also believed that urban densification and compact development allow for the preservation of natural and green areas, which in turn provide better accessibility to parks and green spaces within urban areas, while also providing other

DOI: 10.4324/9781003324409-3

environmental benefits such as improved air quality, wildlife habitats, and biodiversity management. Transport infrastructures play a crucial role in urban densification by improving access to specific locations, reducing public transportation costs, and decreasing the expenses associated with personal travel. Much empirical research has sought to investigate the association between urban density and its impact on these benefits by assessing density in different ways.

A traditional way of measuring density is to calculate the population per unit area: net or gross, where gross uses all area and net takes out streets and other land that is not developable.[1] For net calculation, we used parcel data to remove land being used for transportation, agriculture, open space, water, or land classified as "undeveloped." We also calculated population-weighted density, which weights population in a given area (census block group or tract) by its proportion of population for the city as a whole.[2]

In this chapter, we wanted to relate density to walkscore, park access, transit station access, and zoning. Walkscore, which we obtained by block group, is an estimate of land use diversity that measures the number of amenities within a given distance, weighted by category.[3] For parks, we created a buffer of .25 miles around each block group or tract perimeter, and then calculated the amount of park acreage within the block group or tract and its surrounding buffer. For transit, we counted the number of transit stations that fell within the block group or tract, including the surrounding buffer. Zoning percentages were calculated based on parcel data. We calculated the amount of parcel acreage that was in one of our zones of interest—single-family, multi-family, neighborhood retail, commercial, and public open space—and then calculated each zone type as a percentage of the total acreage in the block group or tract.

Density and accessibility

One can look at density as a continuous variable, and simply relate its distribution to other variables. So, for example, Table 3.1 shows net and gross density by block group, along with percentages of single-family and multiple-family housing, regressed on our three outcomes of interest: walkscore, park access, and station access. What the data shows is that net and gross density appear to lack an association with walkscore and park and station access. For parks, gross density is inversely associated (the more the parks, the lower the density). On the other hand, the percentage of single-family land use is inversely associated with walkscore and stations—which makes sense. Percent multi-family land use is also inversely correlated with stations—which does not make sense.

The above regressions were continuous variables, and given the rather low R-squares, there is obviously a lot more going on. More fruitful might be to group density into categories or clusters. We first used "K-means" clustering, a widely used algorithm to create non-overlapping clusters. The goal of the technique is to minimize the sum of squared distances between the data points.

Table 3.1 Block group regressions

Dependent: median walkscore

Variable	Coefficient	Std.error	t-Statistic	Probability
(CONSTANT)	66.005	1.292	51.095	0
Net density	0.000	0.004	−0.051	0.959
Gross density	−0.006	0.008	−0.717	0.474
Single-family (%)	−0.114	0.019	−5.953	0
Multi-family (%)	0.276	0.024	11.473	0

Dependent: stations

Variable	Coefficient	Std.error	t-Statistic	Probability
(CONSTANT)	3.036	0.217	13.960	0.000
Net density	0.004	0.002	1.641	0.101
Gross density	−0.005	0.004	−1.092	0.275
Single-family (%)	−0.036	0.003	−10.716	0
Multi-family (%)	−0.026	0.005	−5.109	0

Dependent: parks

Variable	Coefficient	Std.error	t-Statistic	Probability
(CONSTANT)	20.535	4.259	4.822	0
Net density	0.083	0.044	1.913	0.056
Gross density	−0.364	0.082	−4.452	0
Single-family (%)	0.031	0.066	0.469	0.639
Multi-family (%)	−0.076	0.100	−0.755	0.450

Figure 3.1 shows how these density distributions are distributed in Chicago, for net, gross, and weighted density. There is a lot of similarity. There is much more density on the north and northwest sides of the city, especially along the lakefront, and much less density on the south side, with exceptions in the southwest and along the lakefront.

Table 3.2 shows the associations between the k-means clusters, for block groups and for tracts, and the three variables of interest. For walkscore, for both block groups and tracts, the results make sense in that the higher the density, the higher the walkscore. For block groups, the association is also mostly as expected, but only up to a point. The highest density category does not have a higher walkscore, whether measured as weighted, net, or gross. For net density, the two highest categories (4 and 5) are unrelated to walkscore.

At the block group level, park and transit access is mostly associated with density—the higher the density, the stronger the association. One exception is that for station area access at the block group level, there is increasingly higher access only up to a point. The highest density category does not have a relationship with station area access.

But at the tract level, these relationships fall apart. There is no positive association between park and station access and density on any

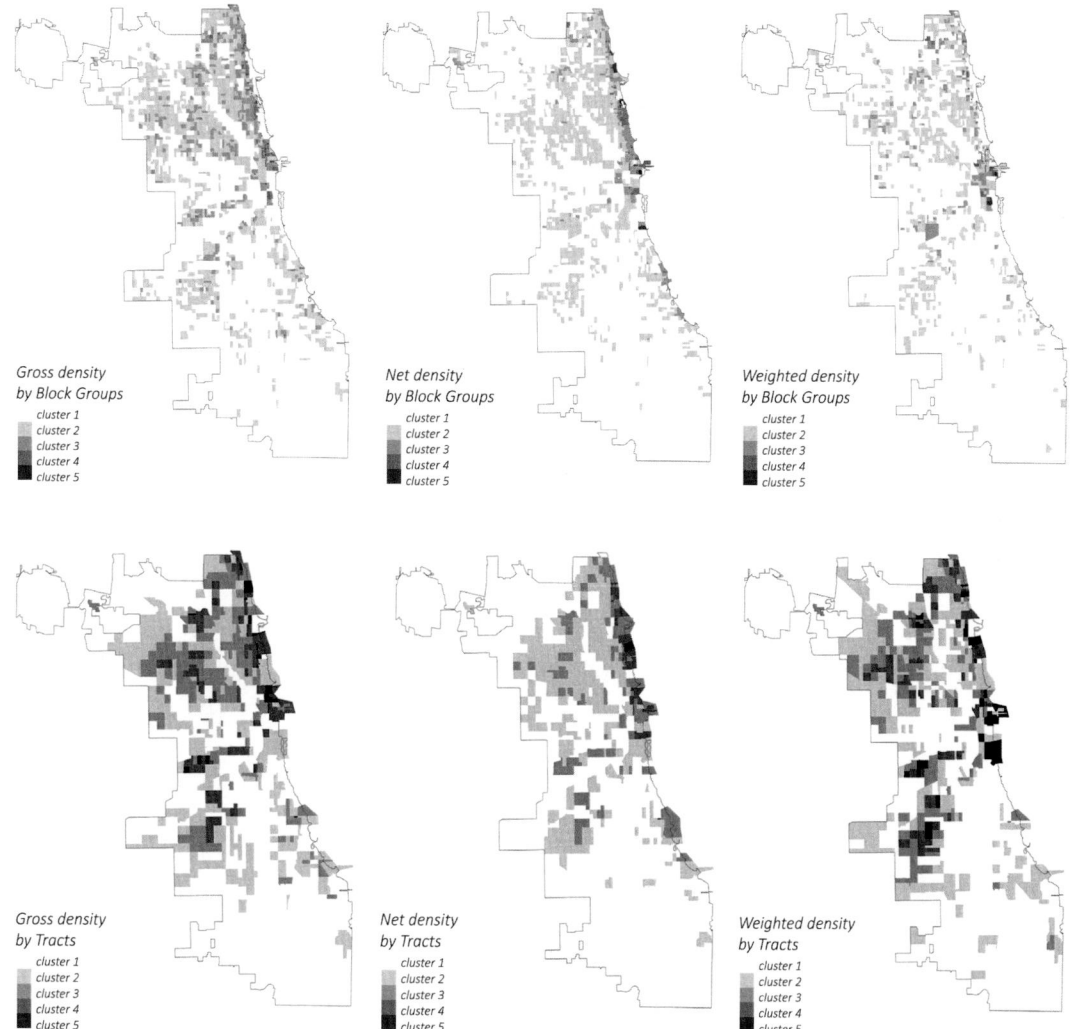

Figure 3.1 K-means cluster maps: by block groups and tracts.

measure. And in fact, park access is mostly negative—the higher the density, the less access to parks. This begs the question: why are tracts negatively associated or unrelated with park and train access, on any measure? The relationships for block groups were better—in the expected direction—but for tracts, there is a lot more that is captured (since tracts are larger), and the relationships are simply less as desired. There is no "proof" that living in a higher density tract yields better access to parks and transit.

Density and zoning

We would expect that density would be related to zoning in some specific ways. First, the higher the density, we would expect there to be a lower percentage of single-family zoning within a block group or tract. Second, the higher the density, we would expect a higher percentage of multi-family zoning within a block group or tract.

Table 3.2 K-means regression results: walkscore, parks, and stations

Block groups

Density	Clusters	Median	Number	Walkscore	Park acres	Stations
Weighted	1	0.7	1478	68	76	1.3
	2	2.4	549	+	+	+
	3	5.5	132	+	+	+
	4	12.0	26	+	+	+
	5	25.6	10		+	
Net	1	27.6	1250	66	54	1.3
	2	64.3	742	+	+	+
	3	138.8	133	+	+	+
	4	286.6	45		+	+
	5	566.8	13		+	
Gross	1	13.9	967	64	66	1.3
	2	31.7	799	+		
	3	54.1	319	+	+	+
	4	112.1	76	+	+	+
	5	223.9	24		+	
						$p > .001$

Tracts

Density	Clusters	Median	Number	Walkscore	Park acres	Stations
Weighted	1	7.5	381	67	16	1.1
	2	22.6	212	+	−	
	3	45.9	119	+		
	4	76.7	61	+		
	5	114.7	26	+		
Net	1	21.9	282	64	17	1.1
	2	43	251	+	−	
	3	68.4	180	+	−	
	4	110.4	63	+		
	5	184.2	19	+		
Gross	1	12.1	286	64	20	1.2
	2	23.7	220	+	−	
	3	38	177	+	−	
	4	57.4	93	+	−	
	5	95.6	23	+	−	
						$p > .001$

These associations are presented in Table 3.3. For block groups, the expected associations with single-family and multi-family zoning are mostly as expected. For all density measures (weighted, net, gross), the higher the density category, the lower the percentage of single-family zoning and the higher the percentage of multi-family zoning.

For tracts it's a different story. Gross density categories 2, 3, and 4 are unrelated to single-family zoning, when we might expect the relationship to be negative. Similarly, net density is unrelated to categories 2 and 3, and weighted density is unrelated for all categories.

Why is there no association between weighted density and either percentage single-family zoning or multi-family zoning at the tract level (with the one exception of weighted density at the highest level having more multi-family zoning)? It is not easy to answer this question, but it does give an indication that zoning is not as determinative as it would seem for increasing density.

We also looked at the association between density and retail zoning. In Chicago, there are two categories of zoning, B1 and B2, that would fit well with—and support—residential density. B1 is a "neighborhood shopping district" intended for retail storefronts on low-traffic streets, with apartments permitted above the ground floor. B2 is a "neighborhood mixed-use district" allowing retail storefronts and apartments on the ground floor. But for block groups, there is no association between these neighborhood retail districts and density in the higher density levels, for any measure of density. For tracts, the association holds, although not for the highest density level.

The association seems clearer for density and commercial zoning, for both block groups and tracts. However, commercial zoning is not as desirable in terms of fitting in with and supporting residential density, since it allows a much wider range of businesses, including liquor stores, warehouses, and auto shops. Still, the basic relationship is that the higher the density, the more the commercial zoning, with the exception of category 2 density (medium-low), and the highest category of density (5) for weighted and net density.

The final zoning piece we analyzed was the relationship between density and the percentage of land zoned for Chicago's parks and open spaces. This is publicly owned land intended for community benefit, so we would expect high density to be associated. In fact, the association is negative or non-existent for all levels, categories, and density measures, for both block groups and tracts.

Alternative density measures: do they make a difference?

Clustering density on four measures

Everything reported thus far has relied on sorting density levels into categories using only one density measure at a time: weighted, net, or gross. In addition, the categorical clustering was used as a type of the k-means algorithm.

Table 3.3 K-means regression results: zoning

Block groups

Density	Clusters	Median	Number	Single-family zoning (%)	Multi-family zoning (%)	B1 B2 business zoning (%)	Commercial zoning (%)	Parks open space zoning (%)
Weighted	1	0.7	1478	54	15	3	9	3
	2	2.4	549	−	+	+	+	−
	3	5.5	132	−	+		+	
	4	12.0	26	−	+		+	
	5	25.6	10	−				
Net	1	27.6	1250	57	12	2	8	3
	2	64.3	742	−	+	+	+	
	3	138.8	133	−	+	+	+	
	4	286.6	45	−	+		+	
	5	566.8	13	−	+			
Gross	1	13.9	967	54	11	2	8	5
	2	31.7	799		+	+	+	−
	3	54.1	319	−	+	+	+	−
	4	112.1	76	−	+		+	−
	5	223.9	24	−	+		+	

p >.001

Tracts

Density	Clusters	Median	Number	Single-family zoning (%)	Multi-family zoning (%)	B1 B2 business zoning (%)	Commercial zoning (%)	Parks open space zoning (%)
Weighted	1	7.5	381	40	18	2	9	5
	2	22.6	212			+		
	3	45.9	119			+		
	4	76.7	61			+		
	5	114.7	26		+			
Net	1	21.9	282	47	11	2	8	4
	2	43	251		+	+		
	3	68.4	180		+	+	+	
	4	110.4	63	−	+	+	+	
	5	184.2	19	−	+		+	
Gross	1	12.1	286	43	12	2	8	7
	2	23.7	220		+			−
	3	38	177		+	+	+	−
	4	57.4	93		+	+	+	−
	5	95.6	23	−	+		+	

p >. 001

There are other ways to cluster and categorize areas based on their density. Instead of using only weighted, net, or gross density, we can cluster on a larger set of variables in an attempt to better capture variation. By grouping tracts and block groups based on this wider range of density-related characteristics, we might be able to account for more nuance in determining different density types and what they are associated with.

We first clustered block groups and tracts on four variables to come up with a new way to characterize density. The variables we combined are: net density, gross density, percent of parcels that are single-family land use, and percent of parcels that are multi-family land use. These variables were used to form five clusters using a technique called "k-medoids" clustering. This is different from k-means in that k-mediods clustering gives less influence to outliers. The objective of the k-medoids algorithm is to minimize the sum of the distances from the observations in each cluster to a representative center for that cluster. The notion of the center of the cluster is more intuitive than k-means because it's an actual observation rather than a composite of different variables that may or may not exist in reality. For this reason, the results are somewhat easier to interpret, as it's possible to identify the actual block group or tract that is the median of the cluster.

Because four variables are used, the resulting clusters are not quite as linearly arranged from lowest to highest density, as with net, gross, and weighted density. Instead, they create types, which we characterize with descriptive terms as follows: post-industrial, suburban, inner-ring suburban, gentrifying or mixed, and lakefront. The categories are the same for block groups and tracts although we use "mixed" as a more appropriate term than "gentrifying" for the tract scale, as it's not as clear that the tracts in that cluster are, in general, gentrifying. Figures 3.2–3.6 show what these different density clusters look like on the ground, and include a map of their distribution.

Table 3.4 lists the resulting densities and land use percentages that make up each group. A few observations can be made. Post-industrial and suburban clusters have the lowest densities, but perhaps for different reasons. Post-industrial areas seem to have a lot of vacant land, whereas suburban areas are simply less dense by way of having mostly single-family houses on single lots. The post-industrial cluster has only 23% single-family land use, whereas the suburban cluster has 62% single-family land use—and yet at the block group level, the post-industrial cluster is lower density than suburban. Also of note is that the lakefront density cluster has significantly higher density than any other category, especially at the tract level. Finally, gentrifying and mixed clusters are much denser than inner-ring suburban clusters, although these differences are not reflected in differences in single-family vs. multi-family land use. This would imply that the gentrifying/mixed cluster is fitting in more people with the same land use profile.

Tables 3.5 and 3.6 present the results of a regression analysis for block groups and tracts. We ran regressions using our three dependent variables: walkscore, park acres within a five-minute walk, and transit stations within a five-minute walk. The explanatory variables are dummy

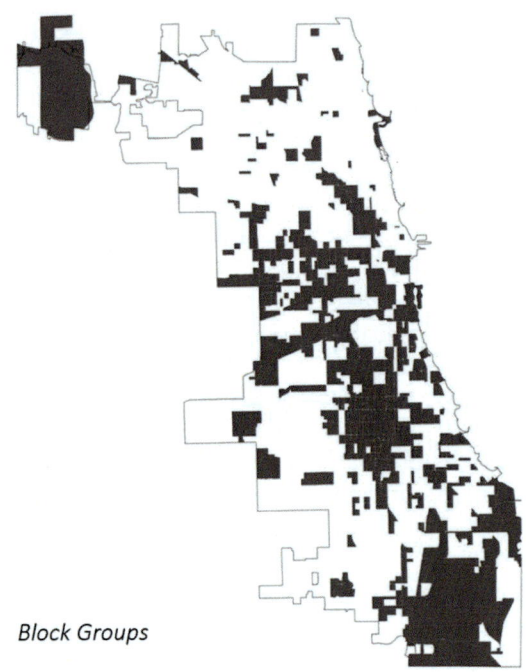

Block Groups

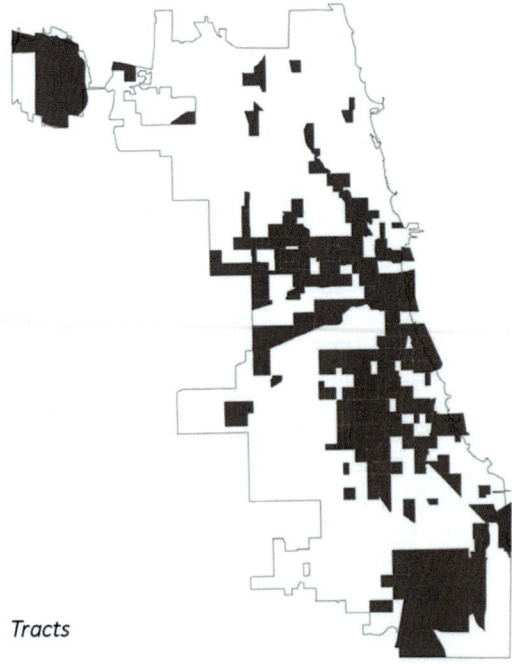

Tracts

Figure 3.2 Post-industrial cluster: older industrial neighborhoods on the South and West sides; small apartment buildings, single-family homes, and vacant lots.

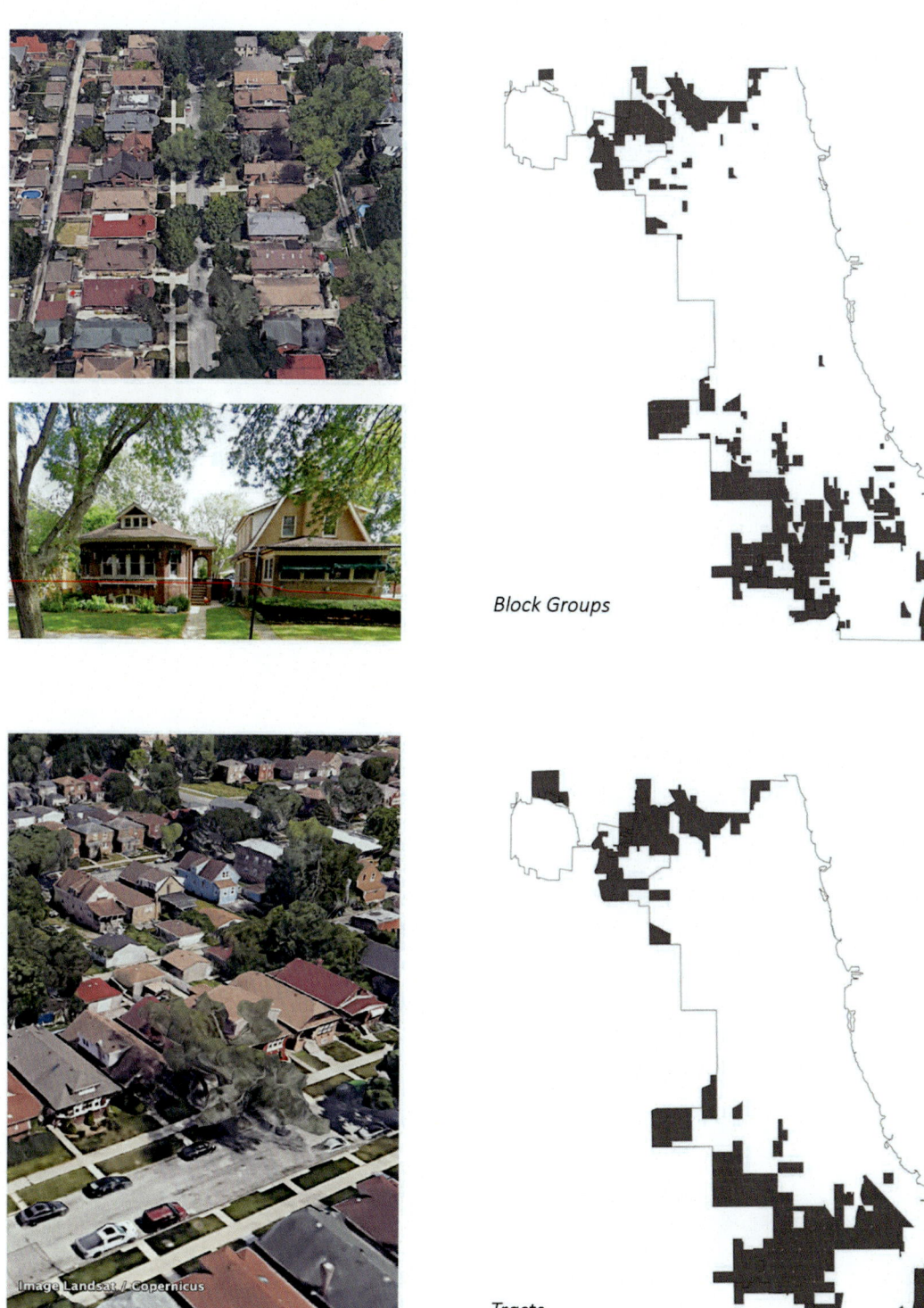

Block Groups

Tracts

Figure 3.3 Suburban cluster: bungalows, ranches, and colonials.

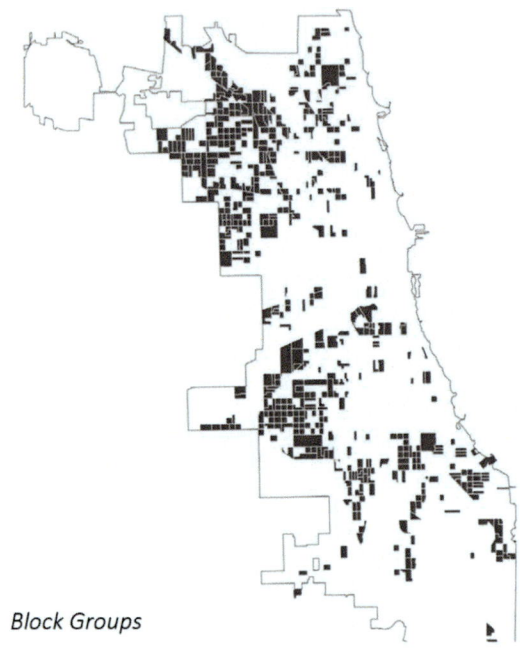

Block Groups

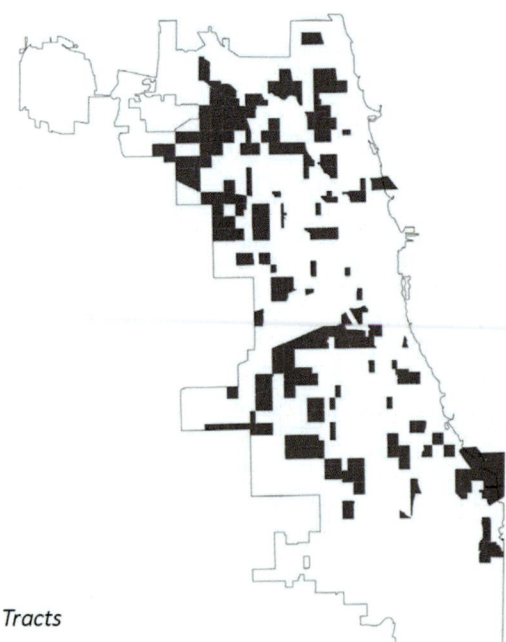

Tracts

Figure 3.4 Inner-ring suburban cluster: diverse housing stock with high social diversity.

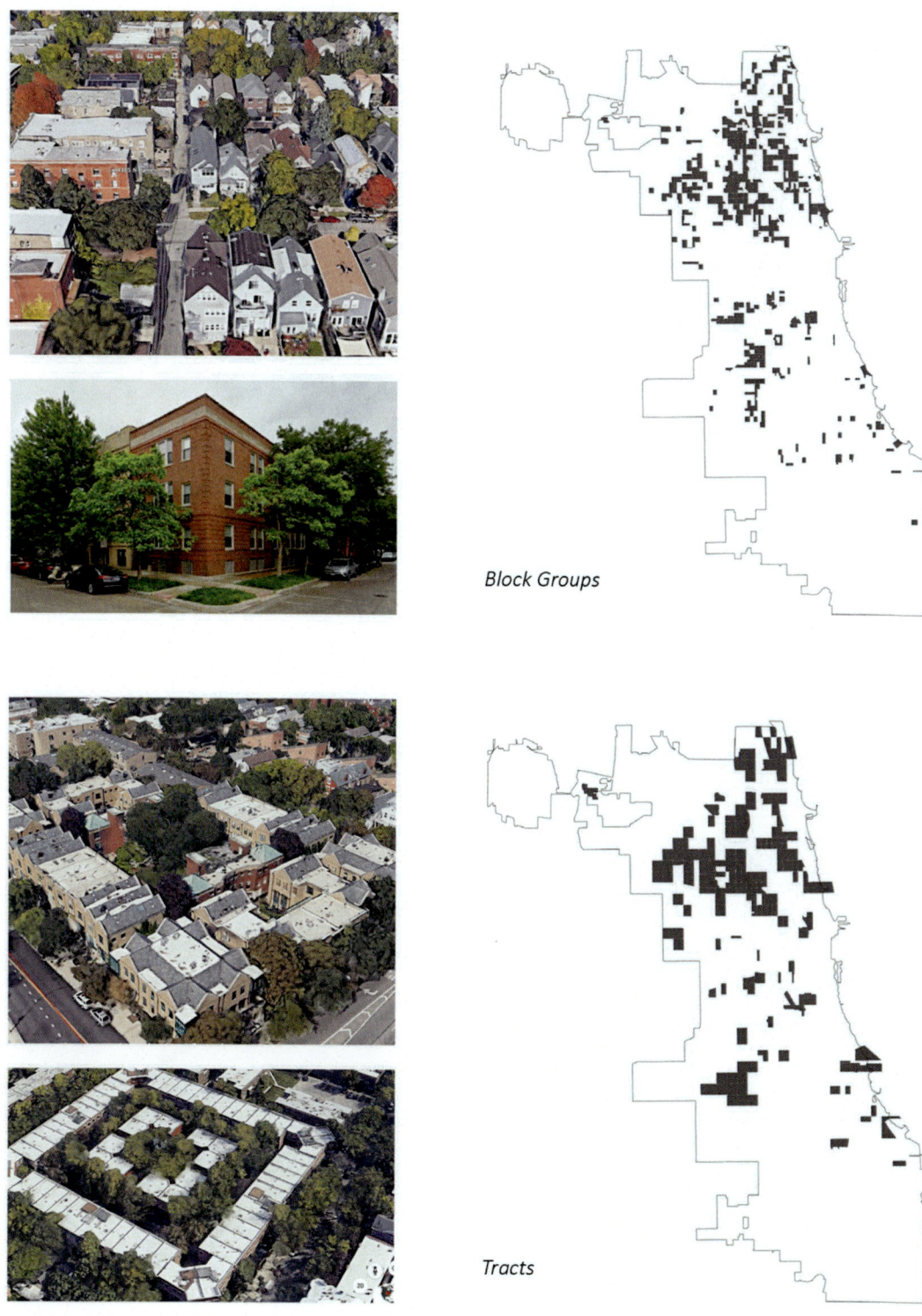

Block Groups

Tracts

Figure 3.5 Gentrifying or mixed cluster: highly diverse building stock, with new investment in apartments as well as single-family and conversions.

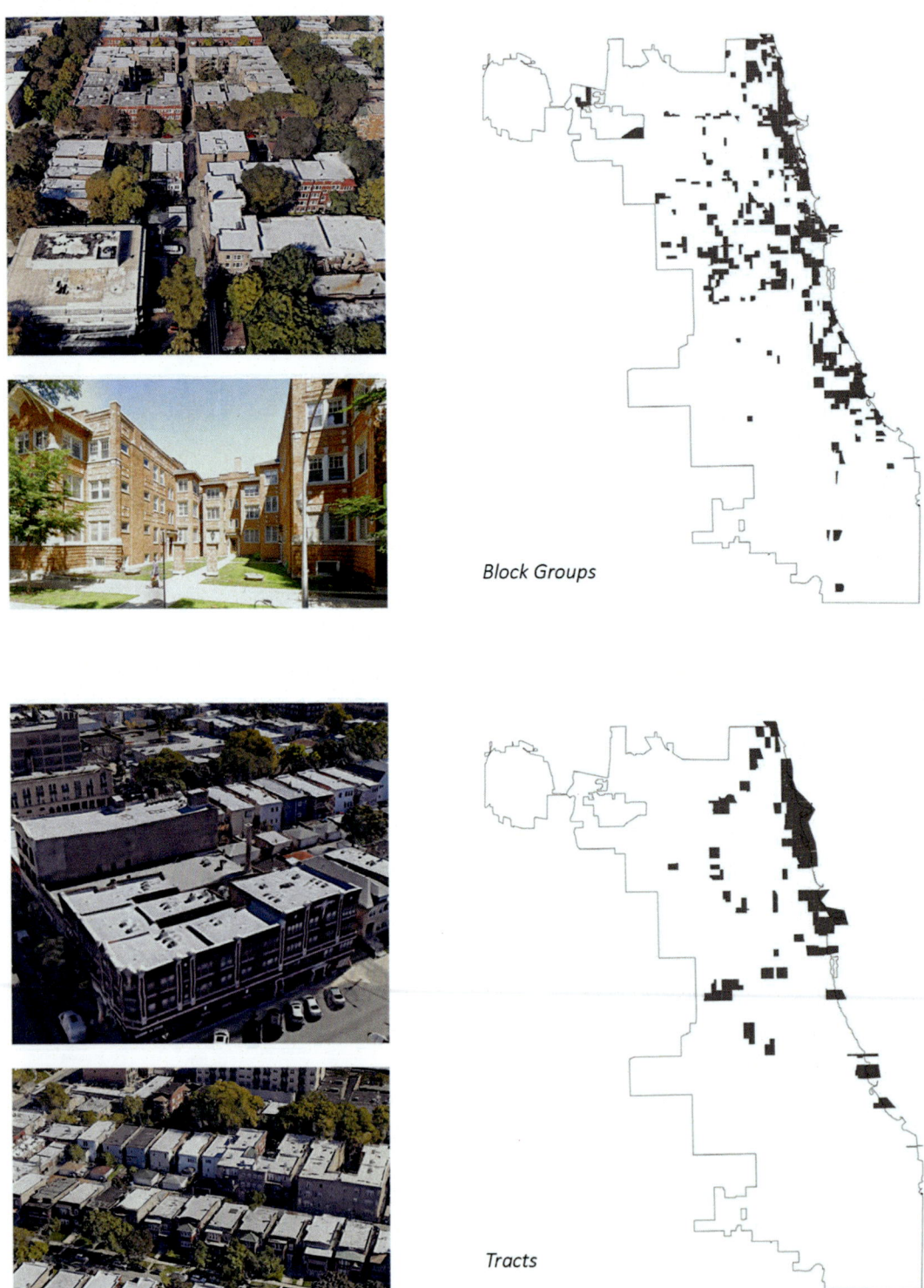

Block Groups

Tracts

Figure 3.6 Lakefront cluster: high rises and apartment blocks.

Table 3.4 K-medoid clusters

Block groups

Clusters	Number	Descriptor	Net density	Gross density	Single-family%	Multi-family%
Base	397	Post-industrial	19.0	12.8	23.1	26.6
1	535	Inner-ring suburban	37.1	24.2	39.0	37.4
2	450	Lakefront	73.5	42.0	13.5	40.5
3	443	Gentrifying	67.5	42.4	35.2	45.5
5	370	Suburban	22.2	14.4	61.9	9.5

Tracts

Clusters	Number	Descriptor	Net density	Gross density	Single-family%	Multi-family%
Base	121	Suburban	19.9	13.0	57.7	12.8
1	197	Mixed	62.1	40.3	34.4	42.4
2	193	Post-industrial	24.6	15.8	20.8	29.4
3	183	Inner-ring suburban	41.3	24.3	37.0	38.0
5	106	Lakefront	107.0	60.6	19.5	46.0

Table 3.5 K-medoid clusters (four variables) and regression results: walkscore, park acres, and stations

Block groups

Clusters	Number	Descriptor	Walkscore	Park acres	Stations
Base	397	Post-industrial	65.3	96.8	1.9
1	535	Inner-ring suburban	+	−	−
2	450	Lakefront	+	+	+
3	443	Gentrifying	+		−
5	370	Suburban	−	−	−
					p >. 001

Tracts

Clusters	Number	Descriptor	Walkscore	Park acres	Stations
Base	121	Suburban	60.1	18.6	0.7
1	197	Mixed	+	−	
2	193	Post-industrial	+		+
3	183	Inner-ring suburban	+		
5	106	Lakefront	+		
					p >. 001

variables on each cluster. For block groups, the post-industrial cluster has the lowest density at the block group level and is used as the base category. For tracts, the suburban cluster has the lowest density and is used as the base category.

As listed in Table 3.5, walkscores are significant and positively associated with every cluster except suburban. The inner-ring suburban cluster does poorly with park access and station access. Gentrifying clusters have no association with parks, and a negative association with stations.

Table 3.6 K-medoid clusters (four variables) and regression results: zoning

Block groups

Clusters	Number	Descriptor	Single-family zoning (%)	Multi-family zoning (%)	B1 B2 business zoning (%)	Commercial zoning (%)	Parks open space zoning (%)
Base	397	Post-industrial	31.9	19.5	2.1	11.8	3.8
1	535	Inner-ring suburban	+	−			
2	450	Lakefront	−	+	+	+	
3	443	Gentrifying	+				
5	370	Suburban	+	−		−	
							p >. 001

Tracts

Clusters	Number	Descriptor	Single-family zoning (%)	Multi-family zoning (%)	B1 B2 business zoning (%)	Commercial zoning (%)	Parks open space zoning (%)
Base	121	Suburban	70.6		1.5	4.4	4.8
1	197	Mixed	−	+	+	+	
2	193	Post-industrial	−	+		+	
3	183	Inner-ring suburban	−	+		+	
5	106	Lakefront	−	+	+	+	
							p >. 001

Cluster 1
Net density: 29

Cluster 2
Net density: 60

Cluster 3
Net density: 71

Cluster 4
Net density: 32

Cluster 5
Net density: 31

Cluster 6
Net density: 20

Cluster 7
Net density: 79

Cluster 8
Net density: 118

Figure 3.7 Density context examples for nine variables clusters.

Figure 3.8 Density context examples for grouped cluster maps.

Lakefront density, the highest density, does well with parks and stations, while suburban, as expected, is negatively associated with all amenities.

The story is different for tracts. Walkscore is positive in all types of density clusters, but the relationship with parks and stations is weak. The mixed-density cluster has negative park access, while the post-industrial has a positive association with stations, but there are no other associations.

Finally, we looked again at zoning and density, but this time using the k-medoids approach to density clustering. The results are given in

Table 3.6. As with k-means clustering, the associations are mixed at best, and often weak. The results that make sense are that (1) single-family zoning is negatively associated with lakefront density at the block group level, and (2) multi-family zoning is positively associated with all forms of density at the tract level, and with lakefront density at both the block group and tract scales. On the business side, there is a positive association between lakefront density and business and commercial zoning.

The results that make less sense are that the inner-ring suburban cluster is negatively correlated with multi-family zoning, and that commercial zoning is positively associated with all forms of density. Small business zoning is only positively associated with lakefront density and the mixed-density cluster (at the tract level). Public open space has no relation to any density type.

Expanding the number of clusters

We wondered what would happen if we expanded the number of density categories from five to eight. Would that make an appreciable difference in relating density to amenities and zoning? We calculated eight density clusters measured in three ways, to see if there were some new kinds of associations, and especially, to see if we could "make sense" of density and its relationships.

We first expanded the number of variables to cluster on, from four to nine, by looking for other ways of measuring density. Previously, we used only net, gross, and percent single-family and multi-family land use for the density clustering. We expanded this to nine variables by adding five scale variables, calculated for each block and then aggregated by tract.[4] We used a 5-category scale typology of buildings: single-unit detached; 2–4 units; 5 units plus, up to three stories; mid-rise/large-footprint; and high-rise. The scale typology number (1–5) was joined to a building points layer, and we then calculated the percentage of buildings at each scale per tract.

With our nine variables, we clustered density into eight categories, and then again ran the regressions using dummy variables for each type of density cluster. Figures 3.7 and 2.8 are images that characterize these different types of density and their spatial pattern. Looking at Figure 3.7, the map shows that the density graduation seems like a fried egg pattern—the downtown ("Loop," Cluster 8) with the most net density, and subsequent clusters fanning out in progressive waves from the center. Figure 3.8 tries to make these results easier to interpret by showing the spatial pattern for clusters grouped by similar net density values. Clusters 6 and 8 stand out on their own, the former being a suburban belt on the outskirts of the city, and Cluster 8 forming the downtown core. Clusters 2, 3, and 7 are a wide mix of housing types, mainly on the north and northwest sides of the city, which are generally considered gentrifying areas. Clusters 1, 4, and 5 constitute a large swath of the south and west sides, which are generally "post-industrial."

Table 3.7 shows the regression results for the clusters shown in the two figures. Walkscore is positively associated for all except Cluster 6, which seems to make sense since Cluster 6 is highly suburban. Parks do not correlate well for any cluster, and negatively with Cluster 3, which is

Table 3.7 K-medoid clusters (nine variables) and regression results

Tracts

Clusters	Number	Net density	Walkscore	Park acres	Stations	Single-family zoning (%)	Multi-family zoning (%)	B1 B2 business zoning (%)	Commercial zoning (%)	Parks open space zoning (%)
1	166	28.6	65	16	0.8	62	6.5	1.8	7.6	3.8
2	123	60.4	+							
3	122	70.8	+	−		−	+	+	+	
4	115	31.8	+		+	−	+		+	
5	98	31.5	+			−	+			
6	85	20.1	−			+				
7	56	78.7	+			−	+	+		
8	35	117.7	+		+	−	+		+	

p >. 001

Table 3.8 K-medoid clusters (gross density only) and regression results

Tracts

Clusters	Number	Gross density	Walkscore	Park acres	Stations	Single-family zoning (%)	Multi-family zoning (%)	B1 B2 business zoning (%)	Commercial zoning (%)	Parks open space zoning (%)
6	99	7	60.2	34.7	1.26	29	9	1	6	8
1	127	39	+	−			+	+	+	−
2	125	30	+	−		+	+		+	−
3	111	22	+	−		+	+			−
4	110	17	+	−		+				−
5	103	54	+	−			+	+	+	−
7	94	13		−		+				−
8	31	90	+	−			+	+	+	−

p >. 001

unfortunate since Cluster 3 has relatively high density with mostly small apartment buildings, and is thus the kind of density that would benefit from park access. Also surprising is the low association between density of any type and transit stations. Only density Clusters 8 (downtown) and 4 (which is relatively low density but is close in to the downtown) have a positive association with transit stations. Multi-family zoning does fairly well with all categories (except the suburban Cluster 6, as expected), but public open space has no relationship with any category.

Table 3.9 K-medoid clusters (net density only) and regression results

Tracts

Clusters	Number	Gross density	Walkscore	Park acres	Stations	Single-family zoning (%)	Multi-family zoning (%)	B1 B2 business zoning (%)	Commercial zoning (%)	Parks open space zoning (%)
4	109	13.5	62	26.5	1.1	35	8	1.5	6.5	5
1	139	24.8		−		+				
2	130	33.5	+				+			
3	117	44.7	+	−			+			
5	104	58.9	+	−			+	+	+	
6	90	71.10	+	−			+		+	
7	68	92.5	+	−			+	+	+	
8	43	142.0	+	−		−	+		+	

p > .001

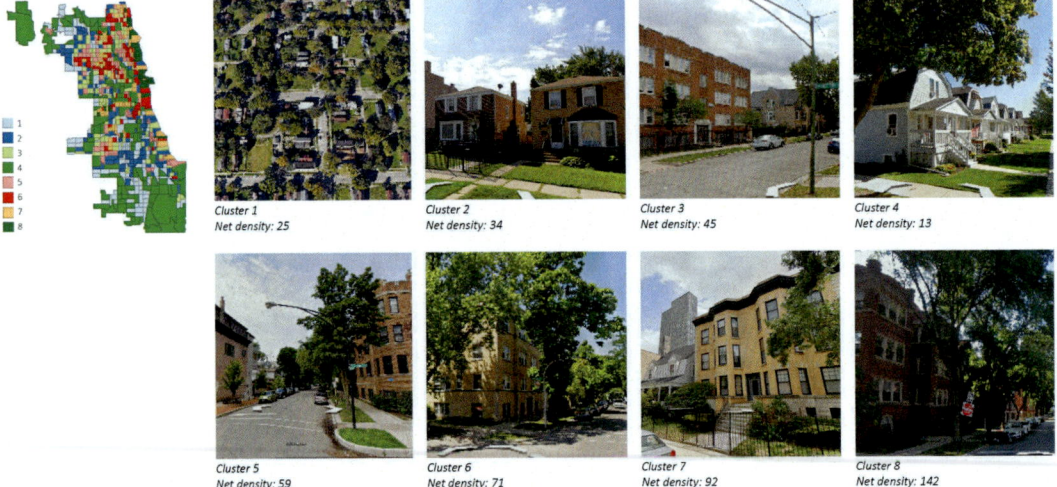

Cluster 1
Net density: 25

Cluster 2
Net density: 34

Cluster 3
Net density: 45

Cluster 4
Net density: 13

Cluster 5
Net density: 59

Cluster 6
Net density: 71

Cluster 7
Net density: 92

Cluster 8
Net density: 142

Figure 3.9 Density context examples for net density clusters.

Associations between parks, stations, and public open space are even worse when we cluster density into eight types using gross density or net density only, as shown in Tables 3.8 and 3.9. Figures 3.9 and 3.10 show the distributions for net and gross density on eight clusters. Although walkscore does well for all categories (except type 7 from gross and type 1 for net), park, station, and open space association are either negative or non-existent at the tract level. Small business retail associations were mixed. Our conclusion is that increasing the number of clusters does not reveal stronger associations between density and amenities.

Figure 3.10 Density context examples for gross density clusters.

Table 3.10 Area deprivation index and density

Block groups

	Median of ADI		Median of ADI		Median of ADI
Category 1 gross density	59	Category 1 net density	56	Inner-ring suburban	49
Category 2 gross density	42	Category 2 net density	37	Lakefront	39
Category 3 gross density	34	Category 3 net density	33	Gentrifying	33
Category 4 gross density	33	Category 4 net density	33	Post-industrial	67
Category 5 gross density	28	Category 5 net density	28	Suburban	50
Using k-means clustering		Using k-means clustering		Using k-medoids clustering on gross density, net density, % SF land use, % MF land use	

Density, deprivation, income, and affordability

Is there evidence that density is associated with socio-economic status (SES)? We looked at the relationships between density and three indicators of SES: area deprivation, median income, and median rent.

We first used an Area Deprivation Index (ADI), measured at the block group level, to investigate the relationship between density and deprivation. The ADI is based on a tool developed by the Health Resources & Services Administration (HRSA) more than three decades ago. It enables the ranking of neighborhoods according to socio-economic

Table 3.11 Tract clusters (four variables) and regression results: income and rent

Tracts

Dependent: tract median income (2020)

Descriptor	Coefficient	Std. error	t-Statistic	Probability
Suburban	68,793.90	3135.79	21.938	0
Mixed	6653.22	3984.07	1.670	0.095
Post-industrial	−22,572.90	4028.65	−5.603	0
Inner-ring suburban	−4908.15	4046.06	−1.213	0.225
Lakefront	−654.94	4588.88	−0.143	0.887

Dependent: tract median rent (2020)

Descriptor	Coefficient	Std. error	t-Statistic	Probability
Suburban	1219.67	37.09	32.880	0
Mixed	143.10	46.76	3.061	0.002
Post-industrial	−144.03	47.47	−3.034	0.002
Inner-ring suburban	−23.57	47.47	−0.497	0.620
Lakefront	145.72	53.68	2.715	0.007

deprivation using a range of variables, including income, education, employment, and home quality. The higher the ADI score, the more the level of deprivation. Table 3.10 shows how the median of the ADI decreases as both gross density and net density increase. This is evidence that there is a benefit to density: higher density is associated with less area deprivation.

However, the last column of the table reveals a slightly different story. Using the k-medoids clustering approach, we looked at the association between deprivation and our five density categories. Gentrifying density, followed by lakefront density, has the lowest deprivation, which is as expected. Post-industrial density fares much worse, and suburban and inner-ring suburban are nearly identical on the ADI index.

What about density and median income? We used median income at the tract level for 2020 (note that median income is not available at the block group level) using our five clusters as explanatory (dummy) variables to see if there is a relationship. Table 3.11 shows that suburban density is the only category that has a positive association with income (using a significance level of $p < .001$). Post-industrial density is the only other significant variable, but it is negatively associated. For median rent, suburban density is the only significant association: suburban density has a significantly higher median rent, but not with any other density type.

We expanded the analysis by regressing the dependent variables of income and rent on eight density clusters—the clusters using nine variables as reported above, and the clusters on gross and net density only. For income, Table 3.12 shows that when density is clustered using all nine density variables, Clusters 3, 6, and 8 show positive and significant association between density and median income above the

Table 3.12 Alternative tract clusters and regression results: income

Tracts

Dependent: tract median income (2020)

Clusters	Coefficient	Std. error	t-Statistic	Probability
Constant (Cluster 1)	48,913.30	2553.03	19.159	0
Cluster 2	11,566.50	3899.81	2.966	0.0031
Cluster 3	39,917.30	3908.93	10.212	0
Cluster 4	3118.80	3986.81	0.782	0.4343
Cluster 5	8779.21	4201.52	2.090	0.0370
Cluster 6	27,596.90	4386.74	6.291	0
Cluster 7	7707.08	5129.64	1.502	0.1334
Cluster 8	47,702.20	6087.62	7.836	0

Tract clusters (nine variables)

Dependent: tract median income (2020)

Clusters	Coefficient	Std. error	t-Statistic	Probability
Constant (Cluster 4)	61,736.60	3410.80	18.100	0
Cluster 1	−6077.85	4526.06	−1.343	0.1797
Cluster 2	−9443.91	4609.98	−2.049	0.0408
Cluster 3	964.77	4698.30	0.205	0.8374
Cluster 5	14,864.70	4835.19	3.074	0.0022
Cluster 6	17,075.00	5020.57	3.401	0.0007
Cluster 7	1152.63	5440.33	0.212	0.8322
Cluster 8	11,696.50	6327.81	1.848	0.0649

Tract clusters (net density only)

Dependent: Tract median income (2020)

Clusters	Coefficient	Std. error	t-Statistic	Probability
Constant (Cluster 6)	55,487.90	3596.17	15.430	0
Cluster 1	24,157.00	4754.61	5.081	0
Cluster 2	14,190.60	4770.86	2.974	0.0030
Cluster 3	1665.75	4909.31	0.339	0.7345
Cluster 4	−2562.69	4930.33	−0.520	0.6034
Cluster 5	11,779.00	4986.02	2.362	0.0184
Cluster 7	5706.85	5113.02	1.116	0.2647
Cluster 8	6308.57	7250.11	0.870	0.3845

Tract clusters (gross density only)

constant. Referring to Figure 3.7, Clusters 1 and 6 are low-density and suburban, while Cluster 8 is in the downtown Loop and is the highest density category in the city. One conclusion is that density and income are related in a way that is bi-modal—high density and low density both have higher median incomes. The association with Cluster 3 is a

Table 3.13 Alternative tract clusters and regression results: rent

Tracts

Dependent: tract median rent (2020)

Clusters	Coefficient	Std. error	t-Statistic	Probability
Constant (Cluster 1)	1039.35	28.49	36.483	0
Cluster 2	130.11	43.67	2.979	0.0030
Cluster 3	438.43	43.77	10.016	0
Cluster 4	141.91	45.00	3.153	0.0017
Cluster 5	88.11	46.76	1.884	0.0599
Cluster 6	249.70	50.17	4.977	0
Cluster 7	224.41	57.50	3.903	0.0001
Cluster 8	825.37	68.27	12.090	0

Tract clusters (nine variables)

Dependent: tract median rent (2020)

Clusters	Coefficient	Std.error	t-Statistic	Probability
Constant (Cluster 4)	1164.66	39.18	29.728	0
Cluster 1	−49.05	51.66	−0.949	0.3427
Cluster 2	−69.30	52.61	−1.317	0.1881
Cluster 3	71.92	53.60	1.342	0.1800
Cluster 5	193.66	55.27	3.504	0.0005
Cluster 6	264.78	57.22	4.627	0
Cluster 7	78.99	61.94	1.275	0.2026
Cluster 8	322.67	71.94	4.485	0.00001

Tract clusters (net density only)

Dependent: tract median rent (2020)

Clusters	Coefficient	Std.error	t-Statistic	Probability
Constant (Cluster 6)	1096.32	41.80	26.227	0
Cluster 1	307.36	54.89	5.599	0
Cluster 2	218.89	55.08	3.974	0.0001
Cluster 3	62.73	56.76	1.105	0.2695
Cluster 4	15.84	56.76	0.279	0.7803
Cluster 5	198.14	57.52	3.445	0.0006
Cluster 7	79.76	59.12	1.349	0.1777
Cluster 8	226.30	83.26	2.718	0.0067

Tract clusters (gross density only)

bit more difficult to interpret, although it is possible that these tracts are gentrifying.

Suburban density Cluster 1 is positively and significantly associated with income above the constant when based on gross density only (Table 3.12). This is true of Clusters 5 and 6 at the net density level as well. But Cluster

8 (high density) loses the association with income when measured as gross or net density. Perhaps it is the suburban association with income that is the most robust.

Finally, we looked at median rent levels using the eight clusters. Table 3.13 shows that when density is clustered using all nine density variables, Clusters 3 and 6–8 show positive and significant association (above the constant, Cluster 1) between density and median rent. For net density, Clusters 5, 6, and 8 have a significantly higher median rent than the constant (Cluster 4). For gross density, Clusters 1, 2, and 5 have a significantly higher median rent than the constant (Cluster 6). Recall that the constants in all cases are the lowest density clusters, so the overall conclusion is that the higher the density, the less the affordability.

Does density make sense?

This exploration of density patterns in the city of Chicago raises important questions about the conventional assumptions regarding the relationship between density and urban amenities. Our goal was to try to answer a fundamental query: does density make sense in terms of providing better services, amenities, park access, transit availability, and SES? Do the regulations imposed support these associations?

The analysis utilized various density calculations, including net, gross, and weighted density, and examined multiple variables such as land use diversity (walkscore), park access, transit station access, and zoning regulations. Perhaps our most significant finding was the lack of a straightforward association between density and urban amenities. Contrary to expectations, higher density areas did not consistently offer superior access to parks, transit stations, or greater walkability. The study also revealed complex relationships between density and zoning regulations, challenging the assumed connections between zoning types and density levels.

Even with increased granularity in clustering, the study failed to identify strong associations between density categories and amenities, suggesting that density is not a particularly strong determinant of urban quality.

On the socio-economic side, while higher density was associated with lower area deprivation, the relationship between density and median income proved to be complex. High- and low-density areas both exhibited higher median incomes, indicating a bimodal relationship. Additionally, the study highlighted a concerning trend—higher density was linked to reduced affordability, as evidenced by higher median rent levels in denser areas.

In summary, the research presented here challenges traditional assumptions about the benefits of density in urban areas. While density has often been touted as a solution for enhancing urban amenities and accessibility, the situation in Chicago reveals a more intricate and less predictable reality. The lack of consistent correlations between density and amenities, coupled with the nuanced relationship between density, income, and affordability, underscores the need for a more proactive approach. Simply increasing density is unlikely to guarantee improved quality of life for urban residents—and yet living densely should, in a normative sense, reward people with an increase in access to amenities. The conclusion is not simply that density does not matter—it is that density should matter, and it often doesn't.

Notes

1   The data was obtained from the Chicago Metropolitan Agency for Planning, or CMAP. More information on their land use inventory is available here: https://www.cmap.illinois.gov/data/land-use/ inventory.
2   More information about population weighted density is available here: Ottensmann, John R., On population-weighted density (2018). https://ssrn.com/abstract=3119965.
3   Details on walkscore are available here: https://www.walkscore.com/how-it-works/.
4   The typology was developed through a review of the literature as well as interviews with stakeholders (market and non-profit developers, as well as planners, architects, economists, and other scholars). More information on the scale typology is available in: Talen, E. (2023). The scale of Urbanism. *Urban Science, 7* (3), 87.

Literature cited

Been, V. (1992). What's fairness got to do with it? Environmental justice and the siting of locally undesirable land uses. *Cornell Law Review, 78,* 1001.

Colantonio, A. (2010). Urban social sustainability themes and assessment methods. *Proceedings of the Institution of Civil Engineers-Urban Design and Planning, 163*(2), 79–88.

Cuthill, M. (2010). Strengthening the 'social' in sustainable development: Developing a conceptual framework for social sustainability in a rapid urban growth region in Australia. *Sustainable Development, 18*(6), 362–373.

Haar, C. M., & Fessler, D. W. (1986). *The wrong side of the tracks: A revolutionary rediscovery of the common law tradition of fairness in the struggle against inequality.* New York: Simon & Schuster.

McKenzie, S. (2004). Social sustainability: Towards some definitions. Adelaide, South Australia: *Hawke Research Institute Working Paper Series 27.*

Ratner, G. M. (1968). Inter-neighborhood denials of equal protection in the provision of municipal services. *Harvard Civil Rights-Civil Liberties Law Review, 4,* 1.

Woodcraft, S. (2012). Social sustainability and new communities: Moving from concept to practice in the UK. *Procedia-Social and Behavioral Sciences, 68,* 29–42.

4

DENSITY IN CONTEXT

Density measures

Urban planners and researchers frequently define urban density as morphological density—the intensity of the built environment in a unit of area. Urban form measures often include fundamental physical elements such as buildings and their corresponding open spaces, plots or lots, and streets (Moudon, 1997). Various empirical studies have explored urban form density and its positive impacts on urbanism goals such as quality of life, carbon emission reduction, and transit-oriented development (Bardhan et al., 2015; Glaeser & Kahn, 2010; Ratner & Goetz, 2013). Urban form density and its advantages are well addressed in contemporary planning movements that advocate Compact City and Smart Growth. New Urbanist advocates "appropriate building densities" and more mixed land-use development. High-residential density is promoted by urban planners as a crucial strategy for Smart Growth. Accommodating public transit and pedestrian-friendly streetscapes are common Smart-Growth principles that minimize the use of private vehicles (Downs, 2005).

The debate on the concept of Compact City and Smart Growth has also focused on understanding sprawl and measuring physical density indicators. Galster et al. (2001) identified dimensions of sprawl such as density, continuity, concentration, clustering, centrality, "nuclearity," mixed uses, and proximity. Ewing (2002) developed four dimensions of sprawl: low-development density, segregated land uses, lack of significant centers, and poor street accessibility. These studies attempted to measure urban form characteristics quantitatively while discussing resolutions for reducing sprawl and promoting Smart Growth.

Population density, one of the major indicators of urban density, quantifies demographic information and demonstrates classifications of urban environments by measuring two numeric components—the number of people and a unit of area. Population density measures are often used to assess their relationship with infrastructure, transportation, commercial, and housing development. The population density pattern is "a crucial economic and social feature of an urban area," but it is claimed that merely considering population density does not fully grasp environmental and contextual characteristics without discussing it in relation to other physical and social features (McDonald, 1989).

DOI: 10.4324/9781003324409-4

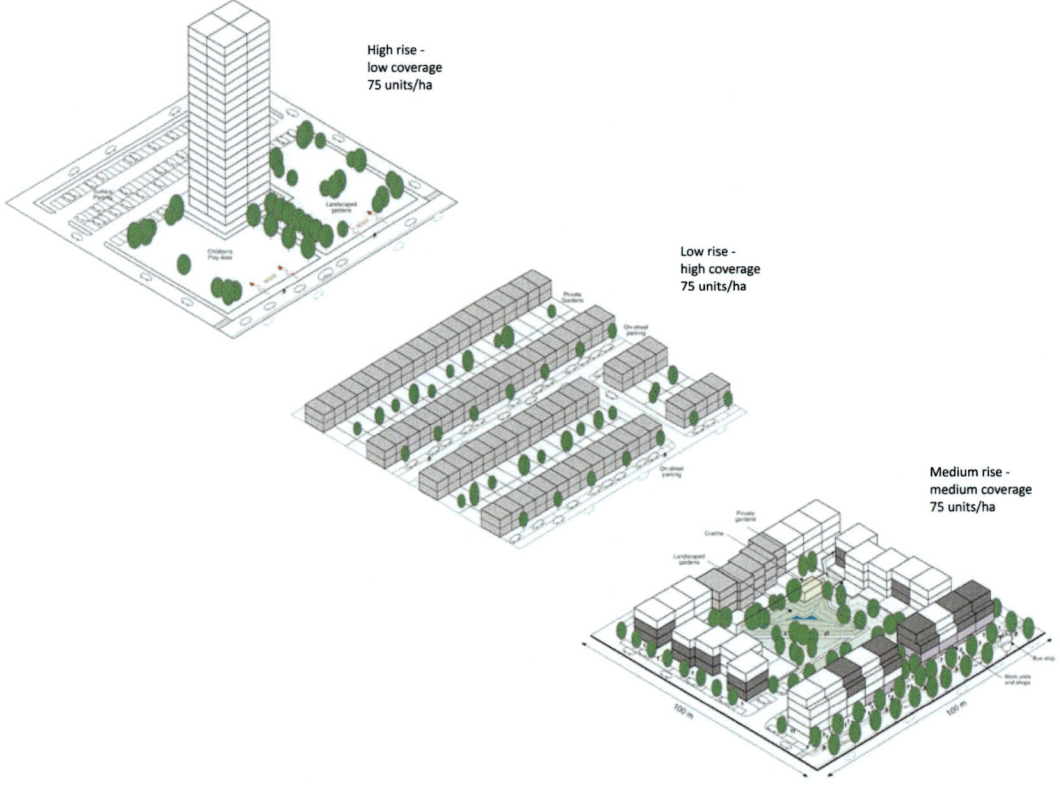

Figure 4.1 Different forms of residential building achieving a same housing unit density (75 dwellings per hectare). (Source: The Urban Task Force, Towards an urban renaissance, 1999.)

Housing unit density measures the number of units in a defined area that is frequently tested by planning researchers and practitioners (Figure 4.1). It is used in descriptions of urban developments as it reflects on how the relevant population could be spatially located. For that reason, vacant housing units are considered in this book to reveal the local trend of housing demand deterioration. It is often associated with shrinking populations (Hollander et al., 2018) which resulted in compromising neighborhood safety, commercial vitality (Accordino & Johnson, 2000), and health (Wang & Immergluck, 2018).

In planning practice, the concept of urban density is imposed in various instrumental and regulatory tools such as land-use restrictions, floor area ratios, minimum lot/house size requirements, and housing unit limits. For example, Euclidean zoning codes have impacted the current density spectrum—from suburban communities with low-density single-family homes to downtown centers with high-density high-rise apartment buildings. FBCs are another regulatory tool that emphasizes the built-form density's role in planning practices. It was designed as an alternative to traditional Euclidean zoning codes which focus more on the *built form* than the type of *land use*. FBC regulates various parameters of built form such as build-to lines, building façade requirements, and street and pedestrian networks.

Reforming planning regulations directly impacts housing affordability. For example, land-use regulation reform could diversify housing types such as multi-family homes and residentially involved mixed-use buildings which likely provide additional affordable and rental housing units in low-density, single-family-oriented neighborhoods (Aurand, 2010). Loosening traditional zoning restrictions might surge housing production which may increase housing density and decrease prices, thus making homes more affordable (Stacy et al., 2023).

In the U.S., housing affordability challenges (e.g., inadequate supply, expensive rental costs) further impact households with low incomes and people of color which, in turn, exacerbates economic and racial inequities (Popov, 2019; Neal et al., 2021). It is concerning that public housing residents live in neighborhoods where access to transport, parks, local services, jobs, and educational opportunities are compromised (Galster, 2013; Koschinsky & Talen, 2015). Additionally, it is particularly challenging to increase the supply of affordable housing in the neighborhood with those desirable characteristics since it became a prominent trend in the U.S. housing market that people prefer living in a walkable community (National Association of Realtors, 2023).

Walkability is an important factor in determining healthy, vibrant urban places (Speck, 2013), reducing the ecological footprint and energy consumption, and minimizing car travel (Van der Ryn & Calthorpe, 1986). Street design attributes impacting walkability such as sidewalks, transit, land uses, street patterns, and trees are considered for the analysis in this book. These indicators have been examined in empirical research. Ewing and Cervero (2010) discovered that walking is strongly related to higher intersection density, land-use diversity, and a higher number of destinations within walking distance. Durand et al. (2011) explored built-environment elements of smart-growth planning and their association with physical activity. They argued that diverse housing types, mixed land use, housing density, compact development patterns, and the amount of open space were correlated with higher levels of physical activity, including walking. Oreskovic et al. (2014) found that the presence of ground-floor windows and street focal points were positively associated with perceived walkability.

Street trees are an essential component of a walkable neighborhood that delineates the pedestrian realm and generates spatial order on streets (Dover & Massengale, 2013). In addition to improving walkability, urban street trees provide economic, environmental, and social benefits to cities and residents. Researchers found that street trees improve air quality (Nowak et al., 2014), increase property values (Donovan & Butry, 2010), decrease pedestrian casualty (Zhu et al., 2022), and aid stress recovery in communities (Jiang et al., 2016). These benefits are equally observed when parks and green spaces are accessible to residents and satisfy community needs. Lack of access to parks and recreational facilities is positively associated with lower levels of physical activity (Diez Roux et al., 2007).

Urban density and its impact on accessibility have been discussed in line with the concept of social equity that aims to accomplish spatial equity

(Deakin, 1999; Talen, 1998; Burton, 2000). It is alleged that urban density benefits residents with various services and facilities in close proximity such as parks, grocery stores, schools, and public transit located near their homes.

Much empirical research has attempted to find different planning strategies to implement urban form density, improve accessibility, and thus, in turn, achieve social equity. For example, zoning and land-use regulations supporting mixed use are considered as an effective planning tool that shapes the built-environment density. Grant (2002) argued that mixed-use promotes greater equal opportunities by increasing access to amenities and job opportunities. Burton (2000) mentioned that residential areas located near retail are particularly important for people with limited mobility and resources such as low-income households, the elderly, and children as it reduces their car dependency on daily routines.

While these benefits are widely acknowledged, high-density urban form has often been blamed for a detrimental effect on social equity. Breheny (1992) mentioned that high-density urban development would negatively impact housing affordability. The cost of land will be more expensive in the Compact City and housing values will be inflated. It is claimed that higher urban density negatively impacts access to parks and open spaces since urban green spaces can potentially be utilized for development (Knight, 1996; Burton, 2000).

The conventional assumption is that density promotes better access to services and facilities, parks, public transport, affordable housing, reduced social segregation and in turn, promotes social equity and other environmental benefits. However, as we discussed in Chapter 3, also as claimed by other urban scholars, there is a lack of consistent correlations between density and better accessibility to amenities proven empirically. In this chapter, we aim to validate these claims on the relationship between urban density and amenities by investigating multidimensional aspects of density.

Why a multidimensional approach?

Urban density, as one of the most crucial characteristics of the built environment, is generally an understandable (Burdett et al., 2004) and self-explanatory concept. Yet the concept of density is descriptive, explanatory, and normative because of "its scientific rationale, its simple mathematical derivation, its apparent comparability, and its possibility for verification" characteristics. In addition, density has a multidimensional nature as it involves various thematic measures (population, housing units), spatial dimensions (blocks, neighborhoods, administrative boundaries), and aggregate functions (net, gross) (Taubenböck et al., 2016). Consequently, it is claimed that density measures and indicators are not consistently accounted for density implication and interpretation.

Rapoport (1975) argued that density is an experiential concept and should be considered beyond the numeric measures such as the number of people and bedrooms per unit area. It is because there are other factors involved in "how individuals respond to other members under specific conditions, previous experience, and social organization." In terms of *perceived* density, Rapoport (1975) explained two major aspects:

1. Relationships among spatial elements (height, spacing, juxtaposition) and environmental qualities (enclosure, intricacy of space, multi-uses, and various activities) may provide very different perceived densities for areas with identical density measures such as people per unit area.
2. Perceived density considers physical elements, and its hierarchy and homogeneity, and social behavioral patterns that affect the levels of social interaction.

These physical and social aspects of density can be evaluated based on various environmental *cues*—temporal, physical, sociocultural—that offer how density is "read" and interpreted. Rapoport (1975) emphasized that density is a complex concept that needs to be understood based on the relationship between various physical *cues* and their impacts on social and cultural factors.

This experiential aspect of density discussed in Tonkiss (2014) involves diverse and spatially contextualized variables such as "mobility as well as dwelling; non-economic uses as well as patterns of employment; spaces we pass through in less purposeful ways, as well as points A to B on the daily journey to work." Tonkiss (2014) asserted that numeric measures (e.g., demographic or employment census data) do not portray temporal and perceptual dimensions of density. It is important to focus on *lived* density that is "produced, experienced, perceived, negotiated, and contested" through people's behavioral patterns (McFarlane, 2016).

Dovey and Pafka (2014) took an integrative approach toward urban density and proposed the concept of density *assemblage* that focuses on the dynamics of relationships among various density measures. The concept of density assemblage is based on the assumption that unpredictable outcomes occur from multiple linkages and connections among social and spatial elements. Density variables related to buildings, populations, and open space were measured and modeled in suburban, urban, high-rise, and informal morphological contexts. The study demonstrated urban density's multidimensional concept and its complexity, emphasizing that "no single density measure or variable can be considered apart from the larger *assemblage*" (Dovey & Pafka, 2014, p. 75).

In this chapter, we considered urban density as descriptive, normative, and relational concept to better understand contextual characteristics of urban density. Urban density is frequently measured by number of populations, housing units, and building density, yet often ignores how these numeric values are related to spatial, environmental, and functional characteristics of cities. By analyzing multiple dimensions of urban density, we aim to discover various ways to leverage the existing density characteristics and reveal what communities need to build sustainable density.

Contextual density typology

This chapter discusses various means of understanding density, focusing on multidimensional characteristics of spatial and functional density. We developed a methodology that creates structural dimensions of density variables and typologies for six cities: Atlanta, Boston, Chicago, Miami, Phoenix, and Seattle. We chose these cities to represent the geographic diversity of cities in the U.S., as well as variations in density characteristics. The study includes 26 density variables that were categorized into five groups:

1. Population and housing density: number of population and housing units per acre, other housing characteristics such as rental, vacant, and HUD-funded housing unit density.
2. Built-form density: gross and net density for building, floor area ratio, and variables associated with block and parcel density.
3. Walkable street density: variables related to walking, biking, and pedestrian safety including speed limit, street trees, tree canopy, bike lanes, sidewalks, street intersection, and cul-de-sac.
4. Land-use density: parcel-level land-use intensity including multi-family residential, single-family residential, big-box commercial, neighborhood-scale commercial, and residential-involved mixed use.
5. Services and facilities density: variables related to neighborhood-scale services and residents' daily needs including bus stops, parks, grocery stores, farmer's markets, and parking.

These density variables were obtained and measured using ESRI ArcGIS software and normalized (mean, value per acre, and percentage) at the census block group level. Table 4.1 includes the data description and availability for the six cities.

Table 4.1 Data availability and variable description

Atlanta	Boston	Seattle	Miami	Phoenix	Chicago	Density variable description	
						Population and housing density	
*	*	*	*	*	*	Population	Number of populations per acre
*	*	*	*	*	*	Housing unit	Number of housing units per acre
*	*	*	*	*	*	Rental unit	Percent of rental housing units
*	*	*	*	*	*	Affordable housing unit	Percent of HUD-funded housing units
*	*	*	*	*	*	Vacant unit	Percent of vacant housing units
						Built-form density	
*	*	*	*	*	*	Building gross density	Building area per acre of the total land
-	*	*	*	*	*	Building net density	Building area per acre of the buildable parcel area proposed for development
-	*	-	-	-	*	FAR	Average of floor-area ratio

Table 4.1 (Continued)

Atlanta	Boston	Seattle	Miami	Phoenix	Chicago	Density variable description	
*	*	*	*	*	*	Block number	Number of blocks per acre
*	*	*	*	*	*	Parcel number	Number of parcels per acre
						Street network and walkability density	
*	*	*	*	*	*	Street intersection	Number of street intersections per acre
-	-	-	-	-	*	Cul-de-sac	Number of cul-de-sacs per acre
*	*	*	-	*	*	Street tree	Percent of street length with trees
*	*	*	*	*	*	Sidewalk	Percent of street length with sidewalk
*	*	*	*	-	*	Lower speed limit	Percent of street length with lower speed limit (≤35 mph)
*	*	*	*	*	*	Bike lane	Percent of street length with bike lane
						Land-use density	
*	*	*	*	*	*	Multi-family Residential	Percent of parcel area that includes attached homes or townhome/condo/ apartment housing
*	*	*	*	*	*	Single-family Residential	Percent of parcel area that includes detached, single-family homes
*	*	*	*	*	*	Big-box Commercial	Percent of parcel area that includes big-box shops, shopping mall or regional shopping center
*	*	*	*	*	*	Neighborhood-scale Commercial	Percent of parcel area that includes neighborhood-scale retail stores
*	*	*	*	-	*	Residential-involved Mixed-use	Percent of parcel area that includes residential-involved mixed use
						Services and facilities density	
*	*	*	*	*	*	Bus stop	Number of bus stops per acre
*	*	*	*	*	*	Park	Public park areas per acre
-	*	*	*	*	*	Tree canopy	Tree canopy areas per acre (including trees on streets and in properties)
*	*	*	*	*	*	Parking	Designated parking land-use area per acre
*	*	*	*	*	*	Fresh food access	Number of farmer's market and active grocery stores per acre

Asterisk (*) indicates data included in this study.

Table 4.2 Results of factor analysis for the six cities (rotated component matrix): density variables grouped in each component showing significant (positive or negative) relationships among them

Atlanta		Boston		Chicago	
Factor/components	*Sig.*	*Factor/components*	*Sig.*	*Factor/components*	*Sig.*
High density with multifamily (F1)		*Form and population density (F1)*		*High density with multifamily (F1)*	
Housing unit	0.903	Building net	0.878	Population	0.910
Parcel number	0.824	Building gross	0.857	Housing unit	0.870
Population	0.808	Housing unit	0.829	Building gross	0.818
Multifamily residential	0.729	Block number	0.827	Building net	0.785
		Population	0.790	Multifamily residential	0.696
		Street intersection	0.769	FAR	0.571
		FAR	0.697	Bus stops	0.393
		Tree canopy	−0.666		
		Parcel number	0.556		
Walkability with vacancy (F2)		*Walkable multifamily (F2)*		*Walkable streets (F4)*	
Block number	0.868	Street Tree	0.842	Street Tree	0.852
Street intersection	0.858	Sidewalk	0.759	Tree canopy	0.781
Bus stops	0.710	Multifamily residential	0.525	Big-box commercial	−0.473
Sidewalk	0.669	*Vacant housing (F8)*		Sidewalk	0.451
Building gross	0.598	Vacant unit	0.717		
Vacant unit	0.512	Park	−0.525		
Bikeable green density (F5)		*Bikeable street (F4)*		*Dense street network (F3)*	
Park	0.737	Bike lane	0.807	Block number	0.746
Bike lane	0.736	Lower speed limit	0.761	Street intersection	0.738
				Parcel number	0.590
				Park	−0.479
Rental and Affordable housing (F3)		*Rental and affordable housing (F3)*		*Rental affordable units with vacancy (F2)*	
Rental unit	0.782	Rental unit	0.788	Rental unit	0.746
Affordable housing unit	0.753	Affordable housing unit	0.707	Single family residential	−0.714
Single family residential	−0.573	Single family residential	−0.673	Affordable housing unit	0.646
				Vacant unit	0.628
Mixed with more parking (F6)		*Mixed use and food access (F6)*		*Neighborhood commercial (F6)*	
Residential involved mixed	0.906	Residential involved mixed	0.759	Neighborhood commercial	0.614
Parking	0.404	Fresh food access	0.691	Bike lane	0.571
				Fresh food access	0.481
Commercial density food access (F4)		*Car-oriented commercial (F5)*		*Less connectivity (F5)*	
Big-box commercial	0.741	Parking	0.786	Lower speed limit	0.723
Neighborhood commercial	0.657	Big-box commercial	0.610	Residential involved mixed	−0.546
Fresh food access	0.627	*Transit commercial (F7)*		Cul-de-sac	0.369
		Bus stops	0.654	Parking	0.328
		Neighborhood commercial	0.653		

Table 4.2 (Continued)

Miami		Phoenix		Seattle	
Factor/components	*Sig.*	*Factor/components*	*Sig.*	*Factor/components*	*Sig.*
Low density pop. and housing (F2)		*High built form density (F1)*		*High built form density (F1)*	
Housing unit	−0.937	Building net	0.833	Street intersection	0.890
Population	−0.887	Building gross	0.782	Block number	0.888
High building density (F3)		Block number	0.716	Building net	0.843
Building net	0.910	Street intersection	0.714	Building gross	0.752
Building gross	0.892	Parcel number	0.673	Bus stops	0.646
		Park	−0.504	Parking	0.546
Walkable, less affordable homes (F8)		*Less walkable but transit accessible (F5)*		*Walkable single-family (F2)*	
Sidewalk	0.656	Sidewalk	−0.337	Lower speed limit	0.813
Affordable housing unit	−0.439	Parking	0.741	Sidewalk	0.742
Connected streets with vacancy (F4)		Bus stops	0.417	Parcel number	0.674
Street intersection	0.887	Bike lane	−0.304	Street Tree	0.633
Block number	0.839			Vacant unit	−0.517
Vacant unit	0.405			Singlefamily residential	0.501
Bikeable to parks and groceries (F6)		*Green density (F3)*		*bikeable and affordable (F5)*	
Bike lane	0.853	Tree canopy	0.884	Bike lane	0.766
Park	0.536	Street Tree	0.832	Tree canopy	−0.541
Fresh food access	0.504			Affordable housing unit	0.469
Rental and multifamily (F5)		*Rental and multi-family (F2)*		*Rental and multifamily (F4)*	
Rental unit	0.749	Singlefamily residential	−0.527	Multifamily residential	0.875
Multifamily residential	0.661	Multifamily residential	0.905	Rental unit	0.665
Big-box commercial	−0.408	Housing unit	0.887		
		Population	0.781		
		Rental unit	0.731		
		Vacant unit	0.542		
Neighborhood scale mixed (F7)		*Groceries and commercial (F4)*		*Mixed with high density (F3)*	
Neighborhood commercial	0.697	Fresh food access	0.783	Residential involved mixed	0.864
Residential involved mixed	0.567	Big-box commercial	0.735	Housing unit	0.753
				Population	0.671
Parking and transit (F1)		*Affordable and commercial (F6)*		*Access to stores (F6)*	
Singlefamily residential	−0.727	Affordable housing unit	0.841	Big-box commercial	0.840
Parcel number	−0.682	Neighborhood commercial	0.520	Neighborhood commercial	0.706
Parking	0.565			Fresh food access	0.523
Tree canopy	−0.558				
Lower speed limit	−0.539				
Bus stops	0.452				

Table 4.3 Results for cluster analysis and descriptive titles for factors

Atlanta	Clusters					
Descriptive titles	*1*	*2*	*3*	*4*	*5*	*6*
High density with multi-family (F1)	**−0.3447**	9.7577	0.2625	**0.4059**	−0.1139	−0.1161
Walkability with vacancy (F2)	0.2630	0.1030	0.0134	**−0.4718**	0.7073	**0.3372**
Rental and Affordable housing (F3)	**−0.4789**	−2.1450	0.0754	**0.8013**	0.5748	**−0.3318**
Commercial density food access (F4)	−0.2219	−2.2444	**3.0258**	−0.2314	−0.8473	−0.2603
Bikeable green density (F5)	−0.2426	−3.3273	−0.0184	−0.0195	−0.4979	**3.3636**
Mixed with more parking (F6)	−0.0287	−0.6519	−0.0267	−0.0587	12.7463	−0.1034
No. of Block Groups (total 289 BGs)	155	1	21	98	1	13

Boston	Clusters					
Descriptive titles	*1*	*2*	*3*	*4*	*5*	*6*
Form and population density (F1)	**−0.4366**	2.5722	0.1981	**0.8595**	0.1430	**0.5613**
Walkable multi-family (F2)	**−0.6537**	−3.2370	0.0970	−0.3802	**0.4198**	−0.0364
Rental and affordable housing (F3)	**0.5726**	1.0471	−0.0051	0.3914	**−0.4382**	**0.6554**
Bikeable street (F4)	−0.1401	2.6974	**2.5693**	−0.1194	−0.2990	−0.0130
Car-oriented commercial (F5)	−0.0514	−0.4858	0.2011	**−0.9108**	0.0612	−0.2290
Mixed use and food access (F6)	−0.1539	−3.7582	0.0282	**5.2250**	−0.0999	0.0515
Transit commercial (F7)	−0.0905	−2.3265	0.0600	**−0.8360**	−0.2206	**3.0653**
Vacant housing (F8)	0.3532	−11.0441	0.0228	−0.4309	−0.1642	−0.0336
No. of Block Groups (total 552 BGs)	179	1	43	11	289	29

Chicago	Clusters				
Descriptive titles	*1*	*2*	*3*	*4*	*5*
High density with multi-family (F1)	**2.8912**	0.2001	0.1092	**−0.8689**	**−0.4682**
Rental affordable units with vacancy (F2)	−0.0373	0.0001	**0.5837**	**0.6960**	**−1.0125**
Dense street network (F3)	−0.3486	**0.6049**	0.2187	**−1.9557**	0.0556
Walkable streets (F4)	**−0.6679**	−0.2532	0.2016	−0.4544	0.0821
Less connectivity (F5)	**1.6820**	**−0.4362**	**−0.3321**	**0.5252**	0.2267
Neighborhood commercial (F6)	−0.1882	**1.5531**	−0.2888	0.4521	**−0.4157**
No. of Block Groups (total 2168 BGs)	109	301	910	194	658

Table 4.3 (Continued)

Miami		Clusters				
	Descriptive titles	*1*	*2*	*3*	*4*	*5*
	Parking and transit (F1)	**1.2704**	**0.4161**	**0.9380**	**−0.4139**	**0.9445**
	Low density pop. and housing (F2)	0.0253	−1.5137	0.4910	0.2678	0.3191
	High building density (F3)	**−1.0281**	−0.2679	**0.8746**	0.1103	**−0.8410**
	Connected streets with vacancy (F4)	**−0.9042**	**−0.5010**	0.2434	−0.1140	**1.6704**
	Rental and multi-family (F5)	**0.5458**	0.2966	**−1.1364**	0.0018	0.3820
	Bikeable to parks and groceries (F6)	**4.1408**	−0.3114	0.5776	−0.1133	−0.2819
	Neighborhood-scale mixed (F7)	**−1.4926**	0.3315	**1.3827**	−0.1631	−0.3411
	Walkable, less affordable homes (F8)	0.2793	−0.2456	**−0.9656**	0.2638	**−0.5777**
No. of Block Groups (total 293 BGs)		7	47	25	187	27

Phoenix		Cluster					
	Descriptive titles	*1*	*2*	*3*	*4*	*5*	*6*
	High built-form density (F1)	−3.6738	0.1071	0.0467	**−0.5765**	**−0.4037**	0.0017
	Rental and multi-family (F2)	7.0521	**1.8882**	−0.3857	−0.4031	0.1203	**0.4708**
	Green density (F3)	3.4083	−0.0021	0.0582	−0.4104	**−0.4165**	−0.0280
	Groceries and commercial (F4)	−2.3760	**−0.3776**	−0.1369	**−1.4278**	−0.0527	**3.2277**
	Less walkable but transit accessible (F5)	−7.6474	0.0485	**−0.2565**	−0.0122	**1.9607**	−0.2316
	Affordable and commercial (F6)	2.4370	−0.1687	−0.0460	**10.3168**	0.0246	0.1168
No. of Block Groups (total 951 BGs)		1	119	684	4	96	47

Seattle		Cluster					
	Descriptive titles	*1*	*2*	*3*	*4*	*5*	*6*
	High built-form density (F1)	−0.0557	−0.8831	**1.9992**	0.1299	−0.2822	**−0.9423**
	Walkable single-family (F2)	**0.4145**	0.1430	**−0.9175**	0.1886	**−2.6611**	**−1.4390**
	Mixed with high density (F3)	−0.1700	14.4589	**1.0184**	0.1383	**−1.4100**	−0.0942
	Rental and multi-family (F4)	**−0.3591**	−0.9680	−0.4584	**1.7912**	−0.9921	−0.0494
	Bikeable and affordable (F5)	−0.2189	−1.5732	**1.4092**	−0.0262	**−1.5377**	**0.3373**
	Access to stores (F6)	−0.0728	−1.2869	0.2704	0.1266	**8.0144**	−0.2992
No. of Block Groups (total 478 BGs)		298	1	36	73	3	67

Note: The bold font signifies the mean component values; these values help in identifying the characteristics of each cluster.

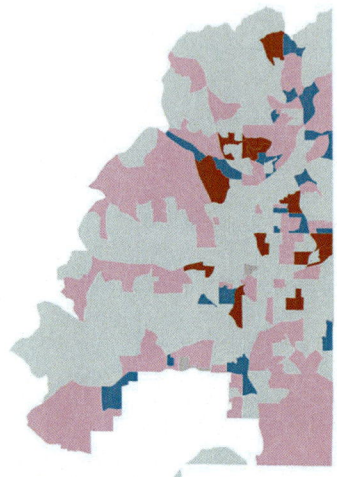

Atlanta

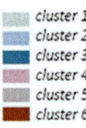

cluster 1
cluster 2
cluster 3
cluster 4
cluster 5
cluster 6

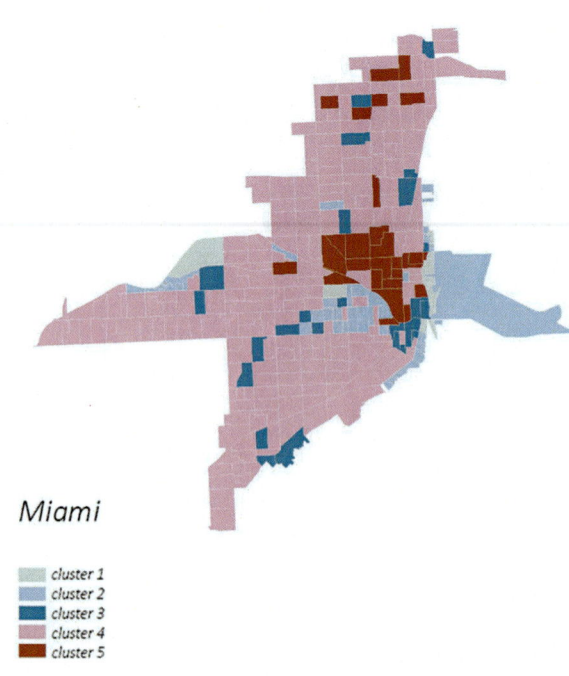

Miami

cluster 1
cluster 2
cluster 3
cluster 4
cluster 5

Figure 4.2 Cluster maps for six cities.

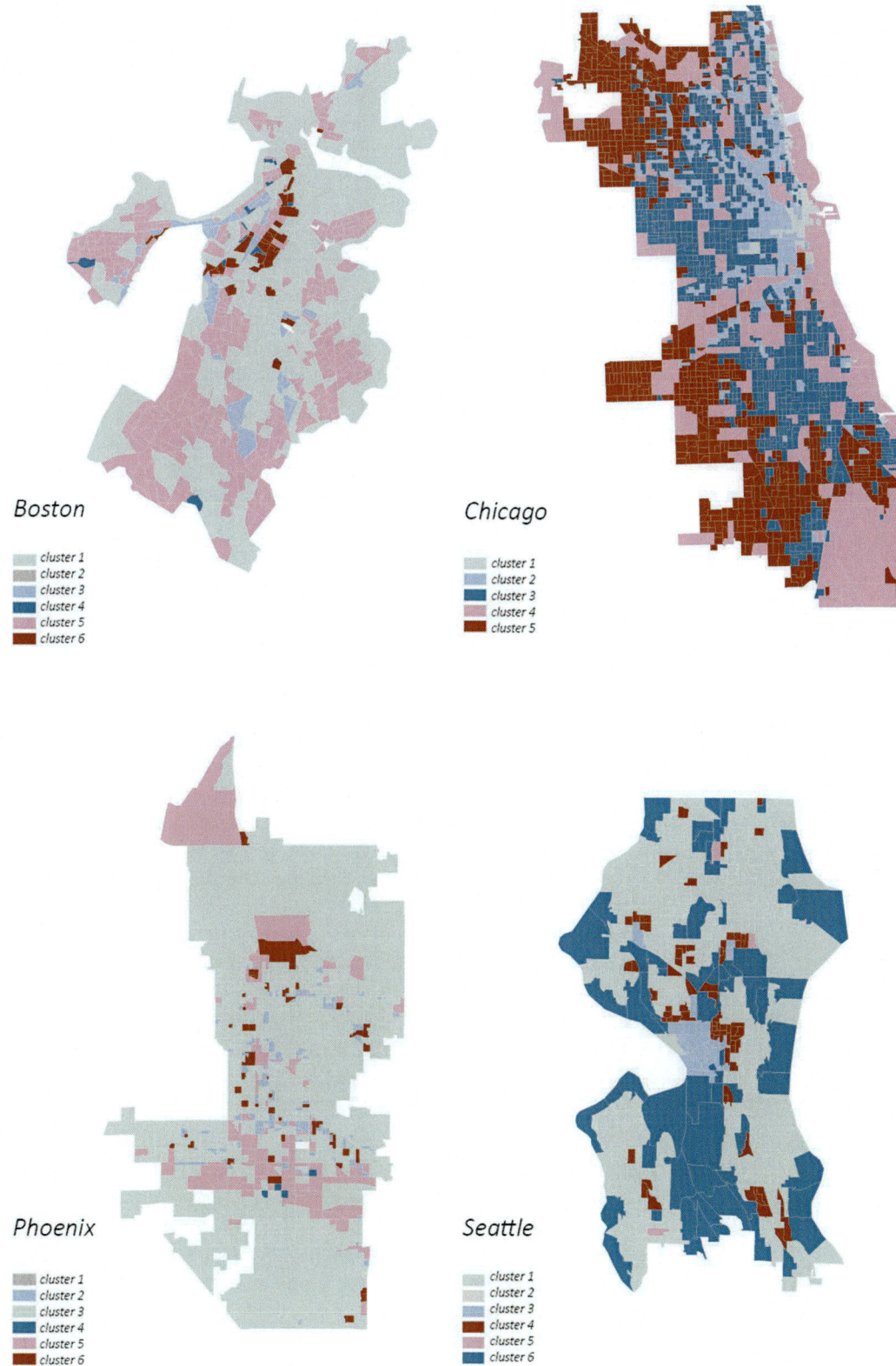

Figure 4.2 (Continued)

We explored the relationship among these 26 density measures using factor analysis; it serves as a descriptive data reduction tool to simplify the complexity of a data set and understand the dimensional structure of density measures. Table 4.2 summarizes the density variables grouped in each component that shares a significant (positive or negative) relationship. Descriptive titles were given based on the characteristics of the variables involved in each factor component. For example, Atlanta has six-factor components of density characteristics: high-population density with more multi-family residential, high-vacant unit density with walkability, rental and affordable housing density, commercial density, bikeable parks, and mixed-use density with more parking. The first-factor component reflects high-population density with more multi-family residential characteristics involving higher housing and population density, a greater number of parcels, and higher percentages of multi-family residential land use.

Cluster analysis was employed to create a spatial pattern of density measures based on the regression factor scores (factor analysis results). Cluster analysis is a method to categorize cases (block groups) that are relatively homogeneous within a group, and heterogeneous between each group. The result of cluster analysis revealed a typology of the density context in each city. We can understand the characteristics of density spatial patterns by interpreting the values presented in Table 4.3. The highlighted regression factor scores on each cluster in Table 4.3 are positively or negatively associated with variables categorized in each factor in Table 4.2.

Figure 4.2 illustrates cluster maps for the six cities that spatially classify neighborhoods based on similar density characteristics. For example, in Atlanta, the block groups classified in Cluster 1 have high single-family residential density with lower multi-family, rental, and affordable housing unit density. In contrast, Cluster 4 offers denser multi-family, rental, affordable housing units in less walkable, less transit-accessible neighborhoods. The following section describes the density characteristics for the six cities and visually analyzes how social, spatial, and functional variables can be used to contextualize density patterns at a neighborhood scale. Some clusters are excluded from the discussion if the clusters involve less than 1% of the block groups with exceptional spatial patterns.

Density characteristics: neighborhood scale

Atlanta

Cluster 1 includes 53.6% of the block groups (155 of 289 BGs) that are dissimilar to *high density with multi-family residential* (−0.3477) and *rental and affordable housing* density characteristics (−0.4789). The block groups classified in Cluster 1 are heavily single-family oriented with lower housing unit density and lower population density. It appears that the Cluster 1 communities have less affordable housing options such as multi-family, rental, and affordable housing units.

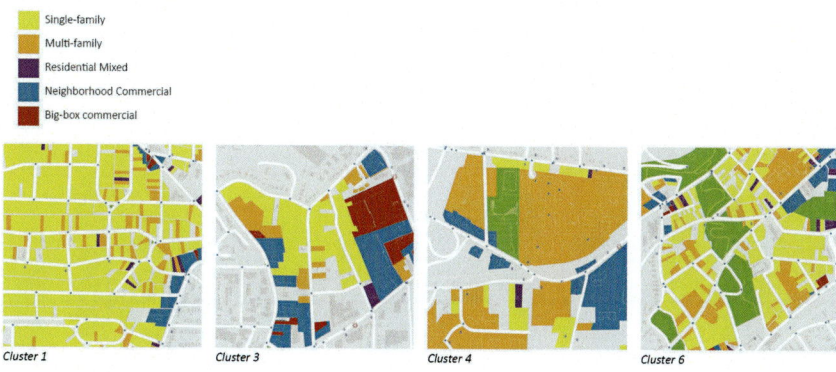

Single-family
Multi-family
Residential Mixed
Neighborhood Commercial
Big-box commercial

Cluster 1   Cluster 3   Cluster 4   Cluster 6

Figure 4.3 Cluster examples in Atlanta.

Cluster 3 includes 7.3% of the block groups (21 of 289 BGs) that are strongly similar to *commercial density with food access* characteristics (3.0285). The Cluster 3 block groups feature commercial land uses such as higher big-box commercial, higher neighborhood-scale retail, and better access to fresh food (grocery stores and farmer's markets).

Cluster 4 contains 33.9% of the block groups (98 of 289 BGs). The characteristics of Cluster 4 are similar to *high density with multi-family residential* density (0.4059) and *rental and affordable housing* density characteristics (0.8013), and somewhat dissimilar to *walkability with vacancy* density (−0.4718). The density characteristics such as higher housing units and population density are observed in the Cluster 4 neighborhoods. In terms of housing options, the neighborhoods in Cluster 4 offer more multi-family, rental, affordable housing units. However, these neighborhoods are relatively less walkable with a lack of public transit access.

Cluster 6 involves only 4.5% of the block groups (13 of 289 BGs) that are strongly similar to *bikeable green density* (3.3636), and dissimilar to *rental and affordable housing* density (−0.3318). The neighborhood classified in Cluster 6 tend to offer more bikeable and walkable environment with better access to public transportation (*walkability with vacancy*, 0.3372) (Figure 4.3).

Boston

Cluster 1 involves 32.4% of the block groups (179 of 552 BGs) that are similar to *rental and affordable housing* density (0.5726), and dissimilar to *form and population* density (−0.4366) and *walkable multi-family* characteristics (−0.6537). It is observed that the Cluster 1 communities offer more options in rental and affordable housing opportunities, but are not supported by population/housing density and walkable environments.

Cluster 3 includes 7.8% of the block groups (43 of 552 BGs). The characteristics of Cluster 3 communities are strongly similar to *bikeable streets* density with low-speed limit (2.5693). These block groups show higher bike land density and streets with slower traffic speeds.

- Single-family
- Multi-family
- Residential Mixed
- Neighborhood Commercial
- Big-box commercial

Cluster 1   Cluster 3   Cluster 4   Cluster 5   Cluster 6

Figure 4.4 Cluster examples in Boston.

Only 2% of the block groups (11 of 552 BGs) qualified for the Cluster 4 category is similar to *mixed use and food access* (5.2250), and *form and population* density characteristics (0.8595). Cluster 4 displays characteristics dissimilar to *car-oriented commercial* (–0.9108) and *transit commercial* density (–0.8360). The Cluster 4 block groups feature indicators such as higher housing unit and population density, residential-involved mixed use, better access to fresh food, but a lack of other types of commercial land uses.

Cluster 5 involves 52.4% of the block groups (289 of 552 BGs) that are similar to *walkable multi-family* characteristics (0.4198) and dissimilar to *rental and affordable housing* (–0.4382). The Cluster 5 communities show equally high density on multi-family residential and single-family residential units with features supporting better walkability, but offer less options of rental and affordable housing.

Cluster 6 contains 5.3% of the block groups (29 of 552 BGs). These block groups show characteristics *of transit commercial* (3.0653), high *form and population* density (0.5613), and *rental and affordable housing* density (0.6554). The density characteristics such as higher housing and population density with rental and affordable housing unit density are observed in Cluster 6. Those neighborhoods are well supported by better access to public transit and neighborhood-scale commercial uses (Figure 4.4).

Chicago

Cluster 1 includes 5% of the block groups (109 of 2168 BGs) that are very similar to *high density with multi-family residential* density (2.8912) and *less connectivity* (1.6820), but dissimilar to *walkable streets* density characteristics (–0.6679). The Cluster 1 block groups feature characteristics such as higher multi-family residential density and higher big-box commercial density, better access to bus stops, and less walkable environment attributes such as lower tree canopy density, lower sidewalk density, and higher parking density.

Cluster 2 involves 14% of the block groups (301 of 2168 BGs) that are very similar to *neighborhood commercial* density (1.5531), and reasonably similar to *dense street network* (0.6049), but dissimilar to *less connectivity* (–0.4362) characteristics. The block groups classified in Cluster 2 involve urban form features related to higher built-form density and

Single-family
Multi-family
Residential Mixed
Neighborhood Commercial
Big-box commercial

Cluster 1   Cluster 2   Cluster 3   Cluster 4   Cluster 5

Figure 4.5 Cluster examples in Chicago.

well-connected streets. The Cluster 2 block groups involve land uses that support services and facilities accessibility such as higher neighborhood commercial density and higher residential-involved mixed-use density.

Forty-two percent of the block groups (910 of 2168 BGs) qualified for the Cluster 3 category, displaying similar characteristics of *rental and afforda-ble units with vacancy* (0.5837) and somewhat dissimilar to *less connec-tivity* (–0.3321). The density characteristics such as higher rental and affordable housing unit density with higher vacancy rates are observed in neighborhoods categorized in Cluster 3. In terms of land uses, Cluster 3 block groups involve low density on single-family residential units and higher density on residential-involved mixed uses.

Cluster 4 contains 9% of the block groups (194 of 2168 BGs). The charac-teristics in Cluster 4 are similar to *rental and affordable units with vacancy* (0.6960) and *less connectivity* (0.5252), and dissimilar to factors related to *dense street network* (–1.9557) and *high density with multi-family* (–0.8689). The Cluster 4 block groups feature indicators such as lower street network density with higher cul-de-sac density, lower population and housing unit density, and higher rental and affordable housing unit density with higher vacancy rates.

Cluster 5 includes 30% of the block groups (658 of 2168 BGs) that are strongly dissimilar to *rental and affordable units with vacancy* (–1.0125) and reasonably dissimilar to *high density with multi-family* (–0.4682) and *neighborhood commercial* density (–0.4157). The neighborhoods classi-fied in Cluster 5 are heavily single-family oriented with lower density on rental and affordable housing units. Cluster 5 is characterized by lower neighborhood-scale commercial density and lower multi-family residen-tial density with sparsely located bus stops and grocery stores (Figure 4.5).

Miami

Only 2.4% of the block groups (7 of 293 BGs) are categorized in Cluster 1, displaying similar characteristics of *parking and transit* density (1.2704), but *bikeable parks and groceries* (4.1408), higher density on *rental and multi-family* residential units (0.5458). In terms of density character-istics, Cluster 1 involves lower *building* density (–1.0281), lower *street connectivity* (–0.9042), and lower *neighborhood-scale commercial and mixed-uses* density (−1.4926). The neighborhoods in Cluster 1 offer rental and multi-family residential units.

Cluster 2 involves 16% of the block groups (47 of 293 BGs) that are similar to *less walkable* neighborhood characteristics (0.4161), and dissimilar to *low population and housing* density (−1.5131) and *connected streets with vacancy* (−0.5010). The Cluster 2 block groups feature indicators related to coarse urban form density such as lower parcel and block density with loosely connected streets. There are higher housing unit and population density along with lower urban form density which resulted in lower vacant housing unit density.

Cluster 3 includes 8.5% of the block groups (25 of 293 BGs). Cluster 3 characteristics are similar to *parking and transit* (0.9380), *high building density* (0.8746), and *neighborhood-scale mixed-use density* (1.3827). The Cluster 3 communities show lower *rental and multi-family* residential unit density (−1.1364) and are dissimilar to *walkable but less affordable homes* density features (−0.9656). There are more affordable housing options, but unexpectedly rental and multi-family residential unit density is also low in Cluster 3. Diverse commercial land uses are observed, but street features (tree canopy, speed limit, and sidewalk) do not support this retail diversity for better accessibility.

Cluster 4 includes 63.8% of the block groups (187 of 293 BGs) that are dissimilar to *parking and transit* characteristics (−0.4139). The neighborhoods classified in Cluster 4 mainly involve single-family residential land uses with higher parcel density. Indicators supporting walkability such as higher tree canopy density and streets with lower speed limit are observed, but these features are not supported by other services and facilities land uses in walkable proximity.

Cluster 5 involves 9.2% of the block groups (27 of 293 BGs). The characteristics in Cluster 5 are strongly similar to *parking and transit* (0.9445) and *connected streets with vacancy* (1.6704), and are dissimilar to *high building density* (−0.8410) and *walkable but less affordable homes* (−0.5777). The Cluster 5 block groups feature indicators that compromise walkability such as lower density of tree canopy and streets with sidewalk. Lower building density and higher vacant housing units are observed along with higher affordable housing unit density (Figure 4.6).

Figure 4.6 Cluster examples in Miami.

Phoenix

Cluster 2 includes 12.5% of the block groups (119 of 951 BGs) that are strongly similar to *rental and multi-family* residential characteristics (1.8882) and dissimilar to *groceries and commercial* uses (–0.3776). The neighborhoods classified in Cluster 2 involve higher housing units and higher population density along with rental and multi-family housing options. It is also observed that Cluster 2 neighborhoods tend to have higher vacant housing unit density with greater proximity to fresh food.

Cluster 3 involves 71.9% of the block groups (684 of 951 BGs). The characteristics in Cluster 3 are dissimilar to *rental and multi-family* (–0.3857) and *less walkable but transit accessible* (–0.2565). Cluster 3 mainly involves single-family residential land uses which resulted in lower population and housing unit density. More sidewalks and bike lanes are observed but streets are not supported by other features related to pedestrian activities.

There are only four block groups (4 of 951 BGs, 0.4%) classified in Cluster 4. The characteristics are strongly similar to *affordable and commercial* (10.3168), and dissimilar to *high built-form density* (–0.5765) and *groceries and commercial* density (–1.4278). The communities in Cluster 4 present high affordable housing unit density. Amenities such as public parks and neighborhood-scale commercials are observed, but with greater proximity of fresh food access.

Cluster 5 includes 10% of the block groups (96 of 951 BGs) that are strongly similar to *less walkable but transit accessible* (1.9607), and dissimilar to *high built-form density* (–0.4037) and *green density* (–0.4165). There are more designated park locations, but lower tree canopy and street tree density are observed. The Cluster 5 neighborhoods involve relatively more parking areas and a greater number of bus stops.

Cluster 6 contains 4.9% of the block groups (47 of 951 BGs) that are strongly similar to *groceries and commercial* uses (3.2277) and somewhat similar to *rental and multi-family* housing units (0.4708). In terms of housing options, the Cluster 6 block groups indicate higher rental and multi-family housing unit density. It is well-served by the greater number of groceries and big-box commercial, but higher vacant housing unit density is observed (Figure 4.7).

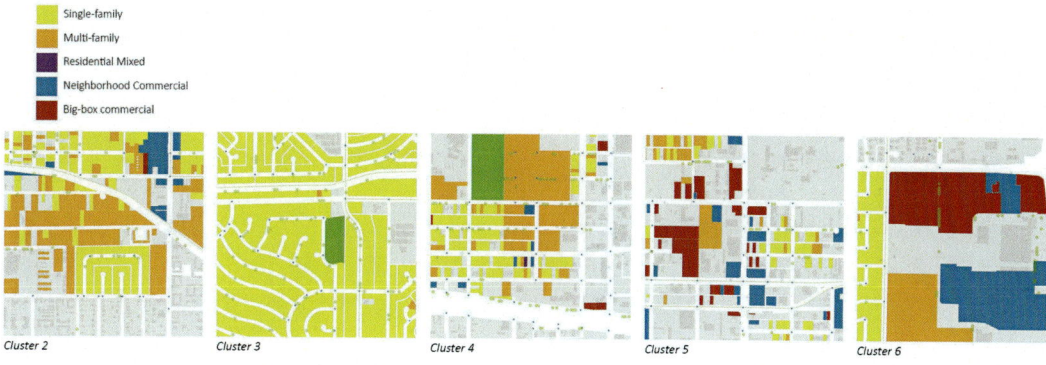

Figure 4.7 Cluster examples in Phoenix.

Seattle

Cluster 1 involves 62.3% of the block groups (298 of 478 BGs). The density characteristics are similar to *walkable single-family* (0.4145) and dissimilar to *rental and multi-family* (−0.3591). The Cluster 1 neighborhoods mainly offer single-family housing options along with walkable street features such as sidewalks, street trees, and lower speed limits.

Cluster 3 includes 7.5% of the block groups (36 of 478 BGs) that are similar to *high built-form* density (1.9992), *mixed with high density* (1.0184), and *bikeable and affordable* characteristics (1.4092), and dissimilar to *walkable single-family* characteristics (−0.9175). The density characteristics such as higher built form and population density are observed. In terms of housing options, the Cluster 3 neighborhoods offer residential-involved mixed use and affordable housing units. Lower walkability and accessibility are observed as there is a lack of street features such as sidewalks, street trees, tree canopies, and streets with lower speed limits.

Cluster 4 involves 15.3% of the block groups (73 of 478 BGs) that mainly offer *rental and multi-family housing* options (1.7912), and are not related to any particular physical and environmental characteristics.

There are only three block groups (3 of 478 BGs, 0.6%) categorized in Cluster 5. The density characteristics are strongly similar to *access to stores* (8.0144), and dissimilar to *walkable single family* (−2.6611), *mixed with high density* (−1.4100) and *bikeable and affordable* (−1.5377). The Cluster 5 areas offer diverse types of retail and fresh food access, but there is no particular housing type observed in Cluster 5.

Cluster 6 includes 14% of block groups (67 of 478 BGs) that are strongly dissimilar to *high built-form density* (−0.9423) and *walkable single-family* housing (−1.4390), and somewhat similar to *bikeable and affordable* (0.3373) characteristics. The Cluster 6 neighborhoods feature lower building density with higher affordable and vacant housing unit density. There is a lack of walkable street features such as sidewalks, street trees, tree canopies, and lower speed limits (Figure 4.8).

Single-family
Multi-family
Residential Mixed
Neighborhood Commercial
Big-box commercial

Cluster 1   Cluster 3   Cluster 4   Cluster 5   Cluster 6

Figure 4.8 Cluster examples in Seattle.

Comparisons

Figure 4.9 describes the comparison between conventional ways of measuring density (population and housing unit density) and the multidimensional approach using spatial analysis. It is observed that some clusters have distinctly different spatial and functional characteristics even if they share very similar numeric density values such as population and housing unit density. Here are some examples:

In Atlanta, neighborhoods categorized in Clusters 1 and 6 have similar average number of populations per acre (7.01 and 7.07, respectively), but their contextual characteristics are dissimilar (Figure 4.10). The block groups in Cluster 1 mainly contain single-family homes and offer fewer affordable housing options such as multi-family, rental, and affordable housing units. The Cluster 6 neighborhoods are more walkable, bikeable, and transit and park accessible, but involve higher vacant housing unit density.

Clusters 5 and 6 in Boston share similar measures in housing unit density (24.88 and 27.03 units per acre, respectively) but their spatial and functional characteristics are quite different (Figure 4.11). It is observed that in Cluster 5 both multi-family and single-family residential uses are equally dominant and spatially integrated within areas. The neighborhoods feature more walkable and accessible neighborhood characteristics, but do not involve rental and affordable housing units. However, block groups in Cluster 6 involve higher rental and affordable housing unit density along with higher built-form density. These neighborhoods have better access to public transit and neighborhood-scale commercials.

Clusters 4 and 5 in Chicago exhibit similar housing unit density values (7.65 and 8.17, respectively) although the neighborhoods offer distinctly different housing options (Figure 4.12). The Cluster 4 neighborhoods involve higher rental and affordable housing units with higher vacancy rates, whereas Cluster 5 neighborhoods involve lower affordable and rental unit density that are associated with higher single-family residential density.

In Miami, as illustrated in Figure 4.13, block groups classified in Clusters 4 and 5 have comparable measures for housing unit density (8.77 and 8.96 units per acre, respectively). The block groups in Cluster 4 mainly involve single-family residential land uses. Indicators supporting walkability such as higher tree canopy density and streets with lower speed limit are observed. However, these areas do not provide walkable destinations—services and facilities—within reasonable proximity. The Cluster 5 neighborhoods involve a greater number of affordable housing units with higher vacant housing density, but street features that do not support pedestrian activities which could make residents living in affordable housing more vulnerable.

Clusters 3 and 4 neighborhoods in Phoenix have similar housing density measures (3.57 and 3.74 units per acre, respectively), but the neighborhoods portray discrete residential patterns (Figure 4.14). Cluster 3 mainly involves single-family residential land uses in walkable neighborhood with more sidewalks and bike lanes, although these neighborhoods do not provide destinations for daily needs within walkable proximity. In contrast, the block groups in Cluster 4 involve high affordable housing unit density with public parks and neighborhood-scale commercials.

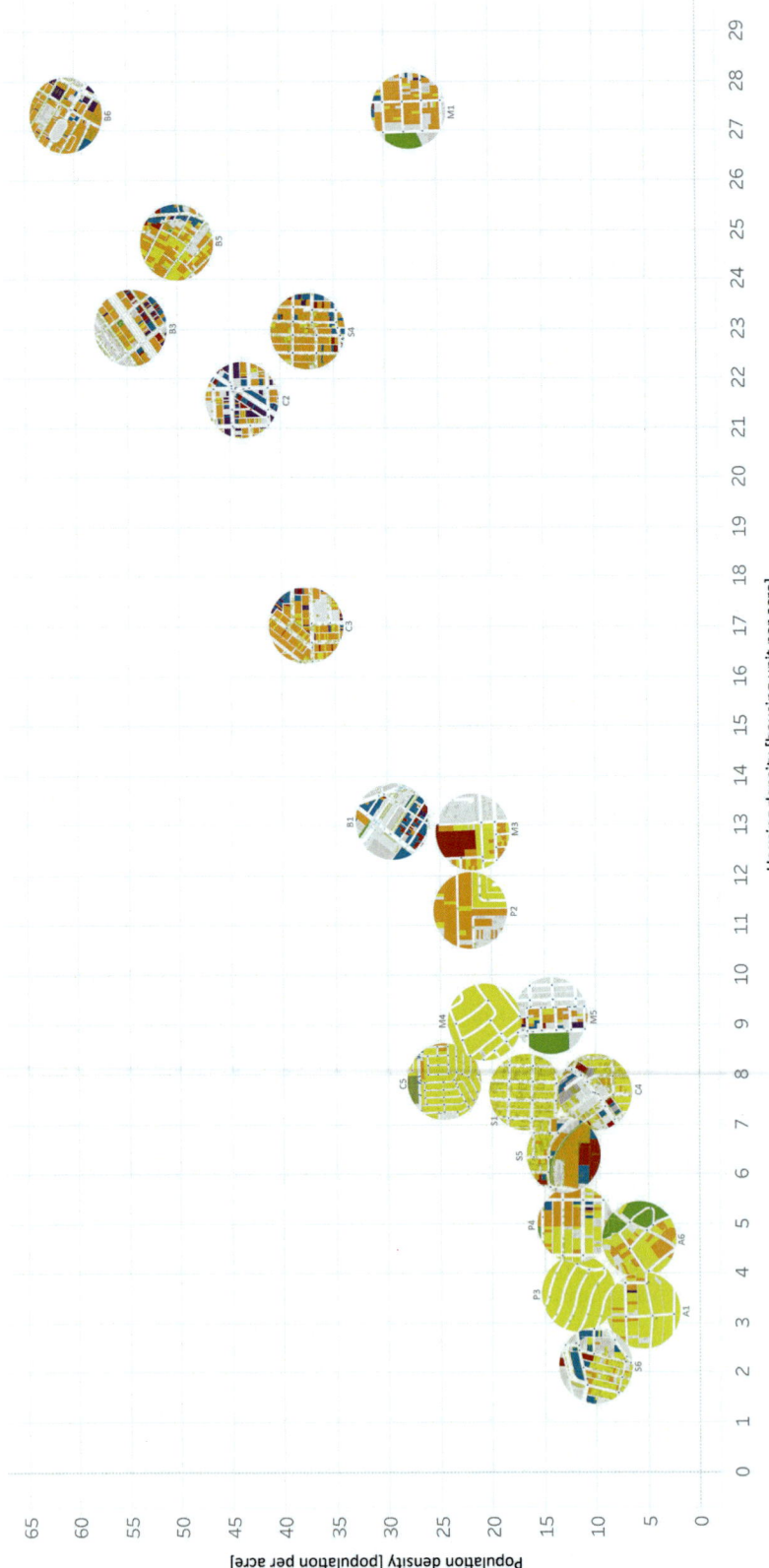

Figure 4.9 Contextual density characteristics and their numeric values for population and housing density.

Figure 4.10 Aerial view comparison between two Atlanta clusters with similar population density.

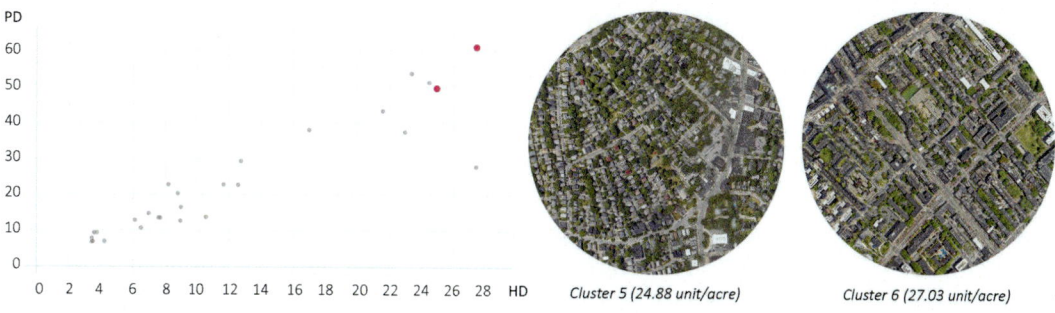

Figure 4.11 Aerial view comparison between two Boston clusters with similar housing unit density.

Figure 4.12 Aerial view comparison between two Chicago clusters with similar housing unit density.

Figure 4.13 Aerial view comparison between two Miami clusters with similar housing unit density.

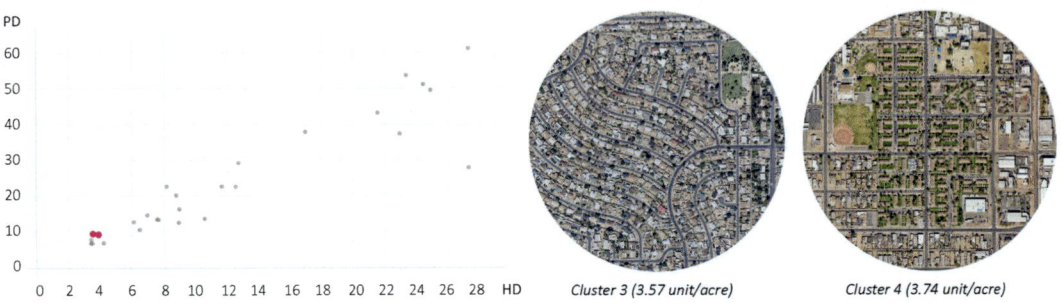

PD
60
50
40
30
20
10
0

0   2   4   6   8   10 12 14 16 18 20 22 24 26 28 HD   Cluster 3 (3.57 unit/acre)   Cluster 4 (3.74 unit/acre)

Figure 4.14 **Aerial view comparison between two Phoenix clusters with similar housing unit density.**

Density in context

In planning theory and practice, it is believed that urban density offers various benefits including better access to amenities, services, and facilities. However, as we explored in the previous chapter, the conventional way of evaluating density does not validate the association between density and amenities. If simply increasing population and built-form density doesn't assure improved quality of life, how might we endorse urban density strategies that respond to local community needs and promote living closer? In this chapter, our goal is to demonstrate an alternative density assessment method that reflects multidimensional characteristics of spatial, environmental, and functional contexts.

This chapter explores contextual density and highlights the limitations of traditional zoning codes used to enforce numeric density regulations through land-use restrictions. It influenced the current urban form density spectrum encompassing low-density single-family homes in suburban areas and high-density high-rise apartment buildings in downtown centers. However, this traditional zoning approach makes it challenging to understand the social and functional aspects of density and its role in representing local preferences and identities.

In Figure 4.15, Atlanta's contextual density map (highlighting Clusters 1 and 4) is compared with a spatial pattern of residential zoning. Atlanta's residential zoning code includes both numeric density regulations and residential types: low, medium, and high housing unit density, as well as single-family residential uses. The spatial alignment between the residential zoning pattern and the contextual density map reflects the existing residential land-use patterns. However, the contextual density map offers additional density characteristics beyond housing unit density and residential land-use information. For instance, Cluster 1 neighborhoods have fewer affordable housing options, such as rental and affordable housing units, while Cluster 4 areas offer more multi-family, rental, and affordable housing units in the context of being relatively less walkable and less accessible to public transit.

Figure 4.16 shows the residential zoning pattern in Boston and how it overlaps with the contextual density map, highlighting Clusters 1 and 5. In Boston, zoning regulations support higher housing density, with the multi-family residential zoning area being twice as large as the single-family residential area. It is noticed that the multi-family zoning areas are divided into two clusters. Cluster 1 provides more options for rental and affordable

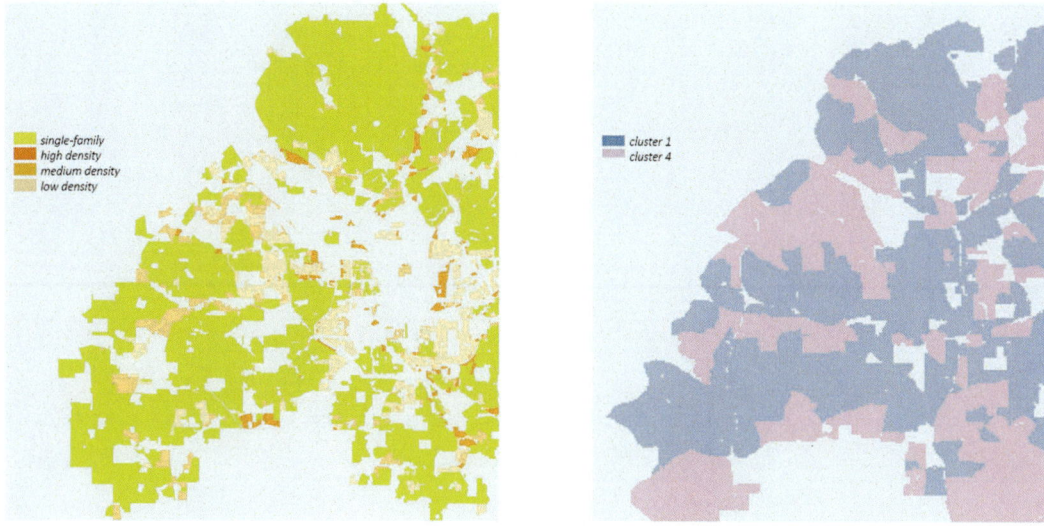

Figure 4.15 Atlanta's contextual density map (right) compared with residential zoning map (left).

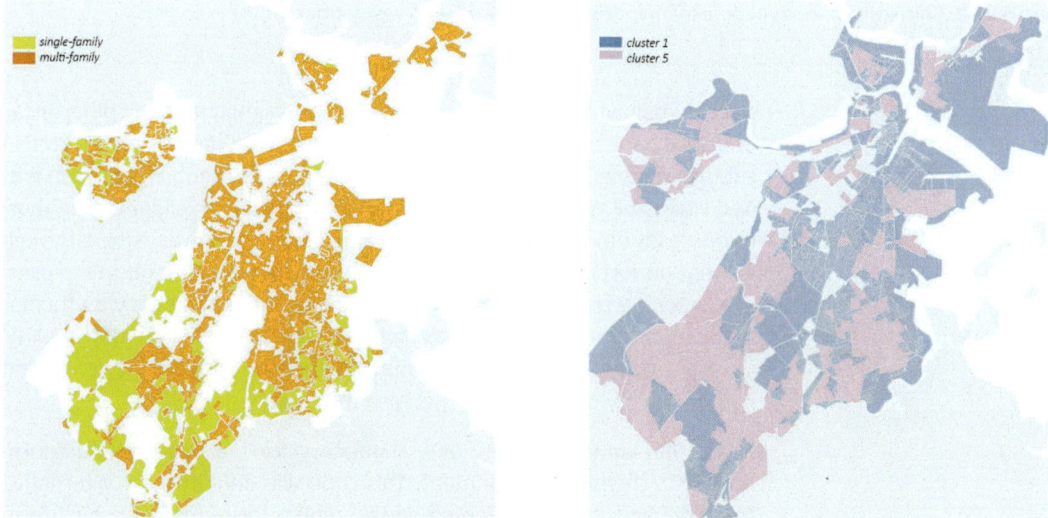

Figure 4.16 Boston's contextual density map (right) compared with residential zoning map (left).

housing, but lacks support from population/housing density and walkable environments. On the other hand, Cluster 5 neighborhoods have high density in both multi-family and single-family residential units, with features that support better walkability. However, they offer fewer options for rental and affordable housing. Clusters 1 and 5 neighborhoods are regulated under the same land-use category of multi-family residential, with the expectation that it would increase population and housing density. However, the contextual density map reveals that they don't share similar characteristics and values related to housing affordability and walkability.

In Chicago, the majority of residential parcels are zoned for detached single-family homes (78%), although the contextual density map does not spatially align with this zoning. Figure 4.17 compares Chicago's contextual

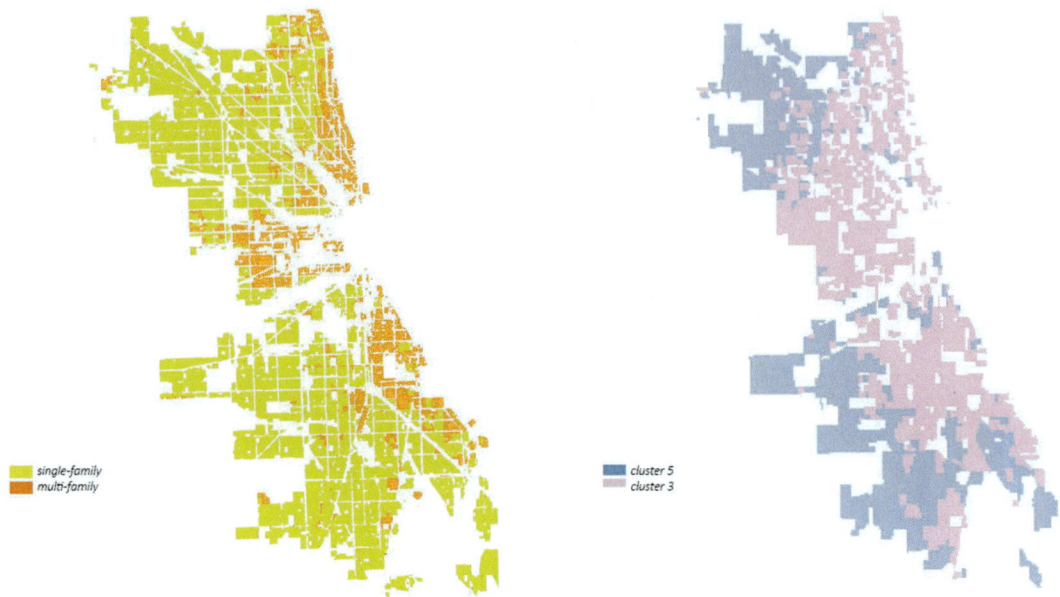

single-family
multi-family

cluster 5
cluster 3

Figure 4.17 Chicago's contextual density map (right) compared with residential zoning map (left).

density map with the residential zoning map, highlighting the differences in spatial patterns. Neighborhoods categorized as Cluster 5 are located in suburban areas, mainly involving single-family residential uses with limited accessibility to services and amenities. Cluster 3 highlights neighborhoods with higher rental and affordable housing unit density, although zoning supports both single-family and multi-family residential land uses. While zoning regulates housing unit density, it does not provide further contextual information such as vacancy rate and housing affordability. Cluster 3 neighborhoods tend to have higher housing vacancy rates and higher density of residential-involved mixed uses.

Miami has adopted a FBC as a regulatory tool to prioritize built-form density in the built environment. This code was created as an alternative to traditional Euclidean zoning codes, which focus more on built-form density rather than land-use type. The FBC in Miami governs a range of built-form parameters, including build-to lines, building facade requirements, built-form density, parking, and landscape standards. In Figure 4.18, Miami's contextual density map emphasizes Cluster 4, while the FBC map highlights T3 zones. T3-zoned areas are classified as suburban, which spatially matches with the Cluster 4 areas. Cluster 4 focuses on single-family residential parcels within a walkable environment, although walkability is not supported by accessibility to other services and facilities in walkable proximity. The FBC in Miami emphasizes contextual characteristics of built-form density, but other parameters are concerned only with the property boundary. To develop locally acceptable density strategies, it is important to consider contextual density characteristics along with form density.

In Figure 4.19, Phoenix's contextual density map (highlighting Cluster 3 areas) is compared with the residential zoning map. The zoning map

Figure 4.18 Miami's contextual density map (right) compared with suburban zoning map (left).

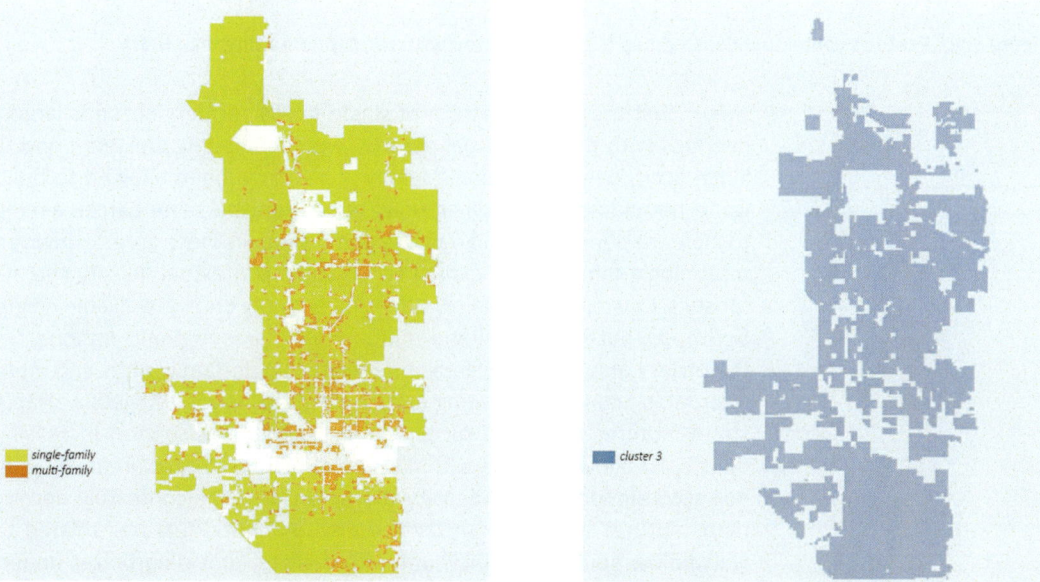

Figure 4.19 Phoenix's contextual density map (right) compared with residential zoning map (left).

shows a dominant spatial pattern of single-family zoned areas in Phoenix, which spatially corresponds with the contextual density pattern of Cluster 3. The spatial alignment between the two maps reflects the existing single-family residential land-use patterns. However, the Cluster 3 map informs other neighborhood characteristics alongside residential types. For example, the Cluster 3 neighborhood offers more walkable and bikeable environments in single-family-oriented areas, but the streets lack support from other features related to pedestrian activities.

In Seattle, the majority of residential areas (81%) are zoned for detached single-family homes, according to the traditional zoning map. Figure 4.20

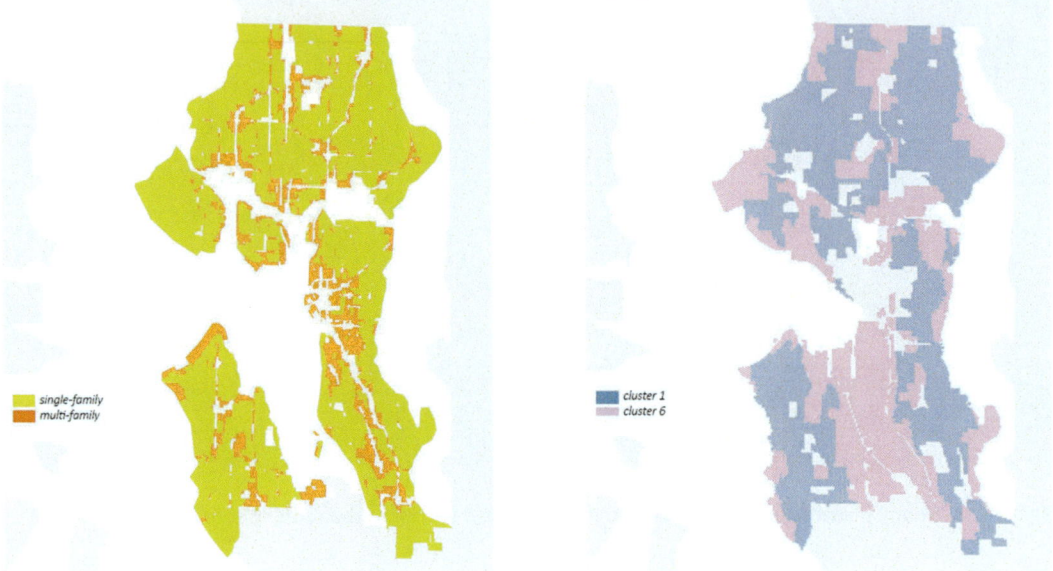

single-family
multi-family

cluster 1
cluster 6

Figure 4.20 Seattle's contextual density map (right) compared with residential zoning map (left).

shows that the spatial pattern of single-family residential zones largely overlaps with the contextual density map highlighting Clusters 1 and 6. Since 2019, designated single-family zones have been allowed to build up to two additional dwelling units (ADUs) on the same parcel, aiming to increase population and housing unit density in these areas. However, most single-family zones exhibit two distinct contextual density characteristics. Cluster 1 areas mainly offer single-family units in walkable neighborhoods, but lack rental and multi-family residential unit options. On the other hand, Cluster 6 areas offer fewer single-family units and more affordable and vacant housing units in neighborhoods with less walkable street features. Although current zoning regulations support increasing density by allowing ADUs within single-family residential areas, they do not accommodate other density characteristics. The contextual density map captures additional social and environmental features related to walkability, housing vacancy, and affordability, providing better understanding of localized density characteristics.

To understand multidimensional aspects of urban density, this chapter provides a methodological framework based on the assumption that certain density characteristics have stronger relationships with localized contexts. We measured a series of urban density indicators for factor and cluster analyses and developed density typologies for neighborhoods in the six cities. This chapter also includes city-scale analysis and mapping ideas to help urban planners and designers initiate urban density visualization and assessment.

The complex relationship between urban density and its spatial patterns and the comparison discussion confirms that the traditional density measures do not grasp cultural, lived, and experiential density. The presented mapping examples in this chapter illustrate how different density indicators contribute to the spatial and functional density characteristics. It also captures what density features are needed to offer more proactive and locally acceptable density strategies for enhancing amenities and better accessibility, and ultimately proposing tangible and feasible ideas for living closer.

Literature cited

Accordino, J., & Johnson, G. T. (2000). Addressing the vacant and abandoned property problem. *Journal of Urban Affairs, 22*(3), 301–315.

Aurand, A. (2010). Density, housing types and mixed land use: Smart tools for affordable housing? *Urban Studies, 47*(5), 1015–1036.

Bardhan, R., Kurisu, K., & Hanaki, K. (2015). Does compact urban forms relate to good quality of life in high density cities of India? Case of Kolkata. *Cities, 48,* 55–65.

Breheny, M. J. (1992). *Sustainable development and urban form.* London: Pion.

Burdett, R., Travers, T., Czischke, D., Rode, P., & Moser, B. (2004). *Density and urban neighbourhoods in London: Detailed report* (No. 13970). London: London School of Economics and Political Science, LSE Library.

Burton, E. (2000). The compact city: Just or just compact? A preliminary analysis. *Urban Studies, 37*(11), 1969–2006.

Deakin, E. (1999). Social equity in planning. *Berkeley Planning Journal, 13*(1), 1–5.

Diez Roux, A. V., Evenson, K. R., McGinn, A. P., Brown, D. G., Moore, L., Brines, S., & Jacobs Jr, D. R. (2007). Availability of recreational resources and physical activity in adults. *American Journal of Public Health, 97*(3), 493–499.

Donovan, G. H., & Butry, D. T. (2010). Trees in the city: Valuing street trees in Portland, Oregon. *Landscape and Urban Planning, 94*(2), 77–83.

Dover, V., & Massengale, J. (2013). *Street design: The secret to great cities and towns.* Hoboken, NJ: John Wiley & Sons.

Dovey, K., & Pafka, E. (2014). The urban density assemblage: Modelling multiple measures. *Urban Design International, 19,* 66–76.

Downs, A. (2005). Smart growth: Why we discuss it more than we do it. *Journal of the American Planning Association, 71*(4), 367–378.

Durand, C. P., Andalib, M., Dunton, G. F., Wolch, J., & Pentz, M. A. (2011). A systematic review of built environment factors related to physical activity and obesity risk: Implications for smart growth urban planning. *Obesity Reviews, 12*(5), e173–e182.

Ewing, R., & Cervero, R. (2010). Travel and the built environment. *Journal of the American Planning Association, 76*(3), 265–294.

Ewing, R. H. (2002). *Measuring sprawl and its impact.* Washington, DC: Smart Growth America.

Galster, G. C. (2013). US assisted housing programs and poverty deconcentration: A critical geographic review. In *Neighbourhood effects or neighbourhood based problems? A policy context* (pp. 215–249). Dordrecht: Springer Netherlands.

Galster, G., Hanson, R., Ratcliffe, M. R., Wolman, H., Coleman, S., & Freihage, J. (2001). Wrestling sprawl to the ground: defining and measuring an elusive concept. *Housing Policy Debate, 12*(4), 681–717.

Glaeser, E. L., & Kahn, M. E. (2010). The greenness of cities: Carbon dioxide emissions and urban development. *Journal of Urban Economics, 67*(3), 404–418.

Grant, J. (2002). Mixed use in theory and practice: Canadian experience with implementing a planning principle. *Journal of the American Planning Association, 68*(1), 71–84.

Hollander, J. B., Hartt, M. D., Wiley, A., & Vavra, S. (2018). Vacancy in shrinking downtowns: A comparative study of Québec, Ontario, and New England. *Journal of Housing and the Built Environment, 33,* 591–613.

Jiang, B., Li, D., Larsen, L., & Sullivan, W. C. (2016). A dose-response curve describing the relationship between urban tree cover density and self-reported stress recovery. *Environment and Behavior*, *48*(4), 607–629.

Knight, C. (1996). Economic and social issues. In M. Jenks, E. Burton, & K. Williams (Eds.), *The compact city: A sustainable urban form* (pp. 114–121). London: E & FN Spon.

Koschinsky, J., & Talen, E. (2015). Affordable housing and walkable neighborhoods: A national urban analysis. *Cityscape*, *17*(2), 13–56.

McDonald, J. F. (1989). Econometric studies of urban population density: A survey. *Journal of Urban Economics*, *26*(3), 361–385.

McFarlane, C. (2016). The geographies of urban density: Topology, politics and the city. *Progress in Human Geography*, *40*(5), 629–648.

Moudon, A. V. (1997). Urban morphology as an emerging interdisciplinary field. *Urban Morphology*, *1*(1), 3–10.

National Association of Realtors. (2023). *The 2023 national community preference survey*. Washington, DC: American Strategies and Myers Research, Strategic Services, LLC.

Neal, M., Choi, J. H., Reynolds, K., Schilling, J., Berger, G., Champion, E., & Young, C. (2021). *Why do households of color own only a quarter of the nation's housing wealth when they compose a third of the nation's households*. Report, Urban Institute, Washington, DC.

Nowak, D. J., Hirabayashi, S., Bodine, A., & Greenfield, E. (2014). Tree and forest effects on air quality and human health in the United States. *Environmental Pollution*, *193*, 119–129.

Oreskovic, N. M., Charles, P. R. S. L., Shepherd, D. T. K., Nelson, K. P., & Bar, M. (2014). Attributes of form in the built environment that influence perceived walkability. *Journal of Architectural and Planning Research*, *31*(3), 218.

Popov, I. (2019). *Housing markets and income inequality*. Apartment List Rentonomics. https://www.apartmentlist.com/research/housing-markets-and-income-inequality (accessed June 2024).

Rapoport, A. (1975). Toward a redefinition of density. *Environment and Behavior*, *7*(2), 133–158.

Ratner, K. A., & Goetz, A. R. (2013). The reshaping of land use and urban form in Denver through transit-oriented development. *Cities*, *30*, 31–46.

Speck, J. (2013). *Walkable city: How downtown can save America, one step at a time*. New York, NY: Farrar, Straus and Giroux.

Stacy, C., Davis, C., Freemark, Y. S., Lo, L., MacDonald, G., Zheng, V., & Pendall, R. (2023). Land-use reforms and housing costs: Does allowing for increased density lead to greater affordability? *Urban Studies*, *60*(14), 2919–2940.

Talen, E. (1998). Visualizing fairness: Equity maps for planners. *Journal of the American Planning Association*, *64*(1), 22–38.

Taubenböck, H., Standfuß, I., Klotz, M., & Wurm, M. (2016). The physical density of the city—Deconstruction of the delusive density measure with evidence from two European megacities. *ISPRS International Journal of Geo-Information*, *5*(11), 206.

Tonkiss, F. (2014). *Cities by design: The social life of urban form*. Hoboken, NJ: John Wiley & Sons.

Van der Ryn, S., & Calthorpe, P. (1986). *Sustainable communities: A new design synthesis for cities, suburbs, and towns*. San Francisco, CA: Sierra Club Books.

Wang, K., & Immergluck, D. (2018). The geography of vacant housing and neighborhood health disparities after the US foreclosure crisis. *Cityscape*, *20*(2), 145–170.

Zhu, M., Sze, N. N., & Newnam, S. (2022). Effect of urban street trees on pedestrian safety: A micro-level pedestrian casualty model using multivariate Bayesian spatial approach. *Accident Analysis & Prevention*, *176*, 106818.

5
DENSITY DIMENSIONS AND PREFERENCES

Density preferences

Measuring the effects of density is complex and the results are often mixed (Talen & Wileden, 2024). Despite this complexity, increased density remains a critically important issue when addressing urban problems and relates to the high cost of housing, the lack of housing options, the need for housing that provides walkable access to services and transit, and the economic, social, and environmental costs of sprawl. This is why efforts to up-zone neighborhoods have gained momentum among planners and policymakers in recent years (Manville et al., 2020).

However, alongside the push for more density, there is vocal opposition (Davis et al., 2023; Whittemore & BenDor, 2019). In response, researchers have tried to better understand how the public views density, especially why residents frequently prefer low-density single-family housing and what could make higher density living more acceptable—and thus, more successful (Trounstine, 2023). The question of density preference—what would make density *preferred*—is a critically important question to answer.

Some opposition to density undoubtedly has to do with the "uncertain social outcomes" residents fear when there is an increase in density (Nematollahi et al., 2016). This appears to be more pronounced among homeowners than renters. As rates of homeownership increase, so too does public opposition to rezoning and preferences for single-family development (Whittemore & BenDor, 2019; Trounstine, 2023). One reason for this is explained by Fischel's (2005) Home Voter Hypothesis which argues that homeowners mobilize politically in response to development they perceive as threatening to local property values. Support for density may be higher among renters because they stand to benefit from increasing housing opportunities, whereas homeowners benefit from housing scarcity. Public acceptance of density has also been shown to vary by resident age. There is evidence that younger people are more open to high-density housing than other, older cohorts (Opit et al., 2020). This raises the possibility that populations overall may grow more accepting over time as renting becomes a more common—and even preferred—option, and as density-accepting younger cohorts replace density-opposed older cohorts.

DOI: 10.4324/9781003324409-5

How density develops has also been shown to be important. In a study of density acceptance in six cities, Wicki et al. (2022) found that both project-related factors and planning instruments have an impact on density acceptance if a project is mixed use, climate neutral, and developed by non-profit investors. These non-design factors—social characteristics and planning process—are important to consider when trying to understand density acceptance.

However, researchers also believe there are controllable form and design matters that can have a significant impact on density acceptance (Park et al., 2019). First and foremost, density requires the right context to be successful and valued. Density, most planners would argue, requires *good urbanism* to thrive and be preferred. Good urbanism is defined as an urban place sufficiently imbued with services and amenities such as public transit and also is composed of a well-designed public realm with buildings that contribute to a pedestrian-oriented context (Campoli, 2012; Parolek, 2020). This perspective—the link between density preference and good urbanism—has become central to planners' views of sustainable cities (Condon, 2020). There is a communitarian emphasis to this ideal: density that is part of a well-designed space can embed housing within a larger context, encouraging residents to "envision each building, each development project, in relation to a positive ideal" (Brain, 2005).

Thus, it is a paradox that researchers have found that community opposition to density often has to do with perceived amenity *reduction*—when additional residents populate an area and density increases, a significant strain besets local amenities such as green space and small business (Bolleter et al., 2021). There might be some truth to this, as researchers have found that density in areas that lack sustaining levels of services and amenities can be counterproductive (Azizi, 2020; Karimi et al., 2020). This is why the "dense sprawl" phenomenon creates the worst of all worlds; it results in density without sufficient close-by amenities and usable open space. The "townhouses" of sprawl are essentially apartments without towns, and are seen as especially tragic since people living in them are forced to live densely without the usual compensations (Calthorpe, 1993).

Fortunately, when density context has been considered where there are services, pedestrian life, and a high-quality public realm, the evidence has suggested that these factors can have a positive impact on density preference (Park et al., 2019). For example, community space, public transit access, and walkability have been shown as necessary accompaniments to new, multi-family development (Billig et al., 2020). Research has also shown that design eliciting feelings of safety and social interaction can have a positive effect, and that these elements are especially present in older, traditionally dense neighborhoods. Unfortunately, some argue that lack of safety and interaction may be lacking in newly dense neighborhoods due to faulty design (Mouratidis & Andersen, 2023).

The link between density and a service-oriented, walkable urban context stands in direct contrast to the last century's views of density. Modernist urbanism, the dominant paradigm throughout much of the 20th century—and still very much a defining quality of modern cities—held that very high densities should be surrounded by open green spaces and highways; the context of density was devalued. The new, radicalized language of modernist city form can be seen in Le Corbusier's scheme for a high-rise city (Figure 5.1) in which virtually all functions are combined into one building. The "Tower in a Park" Model, so disdained by Jane Jacobs (1961), was supposed to be liberating, but it had the effect of separating people from the ground, and therefore their surroundings—a separation that potentially extended to their sense of place, their sense of belonging, and a sense that their individual actions mattered.

This perspective has largely changed, at least from the perspective of planners and urban designers. Over the past several decades, significant writing has focused on design quality in relation to density (Sivam et al., 2012). The books *Visualizing Density* (Campoli & MacLean, 2007) and *Made for Walking* (Campoli, 2012) emphasize the importance of design and argue that density will be valued only if the public understands that density's perceived negative effects—crowding and monotony—are the result of bad design, not density per se. With that in mind, researchers have been trying to understand what might make density more appealing from a building design perspective, which might be particularly important in medium-density development (Navarrete-Hernandez et al., 2022). The importance of historic features, contextual design, visual harmony, and "sensory experiences" have all been noted as important factors in achieving a positive density appraisal (Sotoudeh & Abdullah, 2013; Degen & Rose, 2012; Kyttä et al., 2011; Mousavinia et al., 2019). Developers perceive Millennials as needing density to be authentic, flexible, socially conscious, and supportive of an inside/out, constantly connected lifestyle (Pfeiffer et al., 2019).

A recurrent idea about the best design for achieving density is that it should follow the form of low rise, but dense European cities. In Yanarella and Levine's *Sustainable Cities Manifesto* (2011) the authors argue that the virtues of social connection, urban design and political power are reflected in the typology of the medieval Italian hilltown:

> high population density, a humanly scaled architecture, social heterogeneity, an urban-rural balance, primary political loyalties to the city as a whole, aesthetic richness and diversity of design and social commitment to durability and repair.....[all] critical components of the modern sustainable city.
>
> (Yanarella & Levine, 2011)

The European architect Leon Krier (2009) made a similar case, arguing that cities should be neither "land-scraping" nor "sky-scraping," but composed of compact two- to five-story buildings that are humanly scaled and do not require elevators.

Thus, density in the form of high-rise towers is regularly critiqued in part because it often lacks an appropriately well-designed and well-serviced urban context. It is one reason that Ehrenhalt (2019) described high-rises as a kind of "dystopia." Others have emphasized that high density can be

Figure 5.1 Le Corbusier's "Vertical Garden-City" was density without an urban context: a tower in a park. (Source: Le Corbusier, Concerning Town Planning, 1948.)

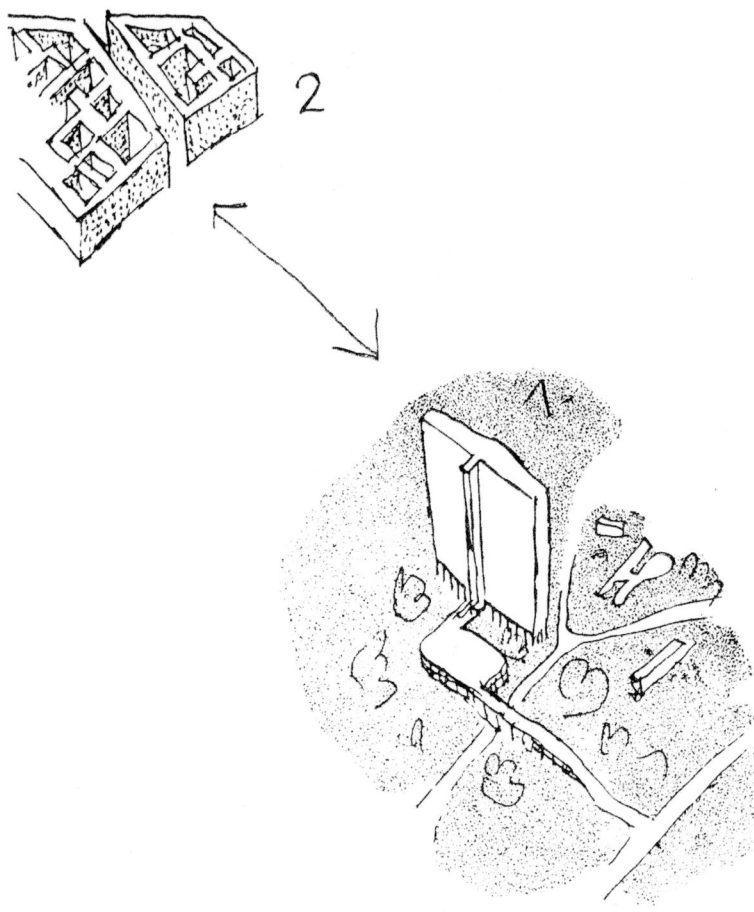

achieved without high-rises and "without having to jump straight into high-rise towers financed by big banks and built by huge development companies" (Price, 2018). So-called "missing middle" housing (often defined as four-to-eight-unit buildings) is higher density housing compatible with single-family neighborhoods, and believed by many to be a more acceptable form of density (Parolek, 2020).

Researchers have also argued that in order to perpetuate support for density, areas around dense and even high-rise development can—and should—be made more child-friendly. The solution is not rocket-science—it can happen by creating additional park space, schools, and easy access to child welfare services (Andrews & Warner, 2020; Thomas, 2020).

However, all of this evidence on how to make density more acceptable—and even preferable—overlooks one consistent and critical finding through much of the density preference literature: people are more willing to say they support density when it is built somewhere else. In their multi-city study, Wicki et al. (2022) found that acceptance of housing densification projects decreased with respondents' proximity to them. Similarly, Hankinson (2018) demonstrated the relevance of proximity in development efforts, finding that while residents in high-rent cities support housing creation in general, they reject proposals to develop housing in their own neighborhood. This support for density in the abstract or in "some other place," but rejection of local density creates a collective action problem—the need for density is acknowledged, but no suitable location can be found.

On the other hand, density preferences seem to be in flux and malleable. It is this fluidity that underlies a sense of hope that if density is well designed—in ways that make it more preferable—density along with its many benefits might be within reach.

Seven density dimensions

Taking the afore-discussed density preference research into account, we selected and proposed seven distinct density dimensions that are likely to impact density preference. Figure 5.2 shows representative images of each dimension. In the paragraphs below, we theorize what these forms of density have to offer, which in turn provides a rationale for why they might make density something to be valued—rather than something to be avoided.

Green density

Green density refers to the concentration and distribution of street trees and their canopies within a dense urban environment. This concept emphasizes the importance of integrating natural elements into city streetscapes to enhance residents' overall quality of life and density acceptance. By incorporating trees and greenery, it is possible to create environments that not only provide aesthetic beauty but also support pedestrian safety and social interaction. The presence of trees can offer

Green density

Integrated transit

Missing middle

Friendly frontage

Communal space

Integrated retail

Historic density

Figure 5.2 Examples representing seven density dimensions.

shade, reduce urban heat islands, and improve air quality; residents feel close to nature despite the urban context. Green spaces and street trees embedded in an adjacent public realm provide a sense of calm and a buffer from what might be perceived as a harsh concrete and asphalt world.

Integrated transit

Integrated transit refers to the strategic placement and accessibility of public transportation within a walkable distance from dense residential areas, effectively integrating the facilities into the daily lives of residents. This concept hinges on the symbiotic relationship between transit systems and surrounding population density. Residents perceive that when public transit options such as buses, trains, and subways are easily accessible by foot, they become a viable and attractive alternative to private car usage, thereby reducing traffic congestion and lowering carbon emissions. Additionally, greater housing unit density near transit hubs ensures a steady stream of users, justifying and sustaining the frequent service of these transit options. This mutually reinforcing dynamic not only makes public transit more efficient and reliable but it also encourages the development of vibrant, densely populated neighborhoods with easy access to amenities and services, fostering a more connected and sustainable lifestyle.

Missing middle housing

Missing middle housing encompasses duplexes, triplexes, townhouses, and other multi-unit or clustered housing solutions that fall between single-family homes and large-apartment complexes. It is also a form of housing that is likely to integrate well with single-family housing, an important aspect of density acceptance. Integrating density in the context of single-family housing provides more housing options and helps address housing shortages in urban areas.

And because of its relatively small size (much more human-scaled than a high-rise, for example), a single block can accommodate a variety of housing types and styles that support different demographic and economic segments and promote inclusivity. Smaller multi-family buildings further enhance diversity by allowing a mix of building types and designs to coexist in close proximity, thus encouraging architectural creativity and innovation. This approach not only enriches the aesthetic appeal of neighborhoods but it also potentially fosters a sense of identity and belonging among residents.

Friendly frontage

Friendly frontage refers to architectural and urban design features that encourage social interaction by creating welcoming spaces along building edges and sidewalks—the space connecting public and private realms. Elements such as stoops, porches, and front gardens serve as transitional zones between private homes and public spaces, allowing residents to interact with their neighbors and passersby in a natural and comfortable manner. These features act as extensions of living spaces where people can sit, relax, and converse—fostering a sense of community and belonging. By providing these semi-public areas, friendly frontages help to animate streetscapes, making them livelier and more inviting. This design approach not only enhances the social fabric of neighborhoods but it also contributes to the safety and vitality of urban areas. Ultimately, friendly frontages create opportunities for spontaneous interactions and strengthen the social bonds that form the foundation of vibrant, cohesive communities.

Communal space

Density that is organized around common space fosters social connections among residents. This is important in dense urban contexts which might otherwise feel impersonal and insular. Common areas create opportunities for people to interact and engage with one another in diverse settings. Common-area spaces serve as gathering points where residents can participate in communal life, thereby strengthening the social fabric of the neighborhood. Communal space might be more formal, providing a structured environment for organized activities and events, or less formal, offering a space for more spontaneous and casual interaction. Ultimately, well-integrated common spaces promote a sense of community, inclusivity, and belonging, enhancing the overall quality of life in residential areas and potentially making density more preferable.

Integrated retail

Integrated retail refers to the strategic placement of small, neighborhood-serving retail in close proximity to related housing. Ideally, this retail would serve daily life needs and ensure that essential services such as grocery stores, cafes, and pharmacies are within residents' walking distance, thereby reducing the need for car travel and promoting a more sustainable lifestyle. The close proximity of retail options encourages pedestrian activity; residents can easily walk to shops and services, leading to increased foot traffic and neighborhood vibrancy. This also fosters social interactions among community members—residents are more likely to encounter neighbors and engage in casual conversations while walking. Moreover, retail integration supports a "live, work, and play" lifestyle by creating dynamic, multi-functional urban spaces in which residents can fulfill various aspects of their lives in one area. It contributes to a more cohesive and connected community where the convenience of nearby amenities enhances the overall quality of life.

Historic density

Historic density involves the preservation and integration of buildings with historical elements that provide significant cultural and historical value to communities. Historic density is enlisted to provide a tangible link to the past, offering a sense of continuity and identity that enriches urban neighborhoods. It is a form of density that contributes to a distinct sense of place and character, making density highly desirable. Historic buildings often tell the stories of a community's development, achievements, and cultural evolution, fostering a sense of pride and belonging among residents. The presence of such structures can also enhance the aesthetic appeal of neighborhoods, encouraging economic development.

Preserving historic density has the added value of promoting sustainable development by repurposing existing buildings, thereby reducing the environmental impact associated with new construction.

Density preferences survey

We used the seven density conditions to conduct a survey of density preferences. Before initiating the main survey, we conducted a preliminary survey by inviting a group of students from the Master of Urban and Regional Planning program at the University of Minnesota to evaluate our seven dimensions. The 12 participating students were asked to identify and confirm the urban density features presented in each photograph. They verified that survey images tended to exhibit more than one dimension, as listed in Figure 5.3. The overall prevalence of the dimensions was given in Table 5.1.

The dimension with the most representation was green density, followed by missing middle housing. About one-fifth of the images included some element of a transit system according to our student respondents.

For the main survey, 186 participants were recruited to represent various population segments (considering age, race/ethnicity, years of education, and household income) currently living in the U.S.[1] The main purpose of the survey was to learn what factors make density more acceptable and desirable. Participants reviewed 24 images of residential buildings and community features involving one or more density dimensions as described above and listed in Figure 5.3. Participants were asked to rate their agreement with the statement, "This is a place where I would like to live," using a Likert scale from strongly agree to strongly disagree.

Respondent characteristics

The first set of questions asked participants about their living environments such as current and previous housing types, presence of multi-family units, stores or transit, parks, sidewalks, neighborhood safety, and the general type of their current neighborhood. A second set of variables asked respondents about individual characteristics such as gender, income, and race. In the main part of the survey, we asked respondents to evaluate 24 images showing various depictions of density.

Table 5.1 Image dimensions

Dimension	No. of images	% of images
Green density	15	63
Missing middle	14	58
Friendly frontage	10	42
Communal space	9	38
Integrated retail	8	33
Historic density	7	29
Integrated transit	5	21

Image 1
Green density
Missing middle
Friendly frontage

Image 2
Green density
Missing middle
Integrated retail
Historic density
Photo credit: Eric Dale
Creative/ Adobe Stock

Image 3
Integrated transit

Image 4
Missing middle
Friendly frontage
Historic density

Image 5
Integrated transit

Image 6
Green density
Integrated retail

Image 7
Green density
Missing middle
Friendly frontage
Photo credit:
missingmiddlehousing.com

Image 8
Green density
Missing middle
Friendly frontage
Communal space
Photo credit: Kristi Blokhin /
Shutterstock

Image 9
Missing middle
Historic density

Image 10
Missing middle
Integrated retail
Historic density
Photo credit:
missingmiddlehousing.com

Image 11
Green density
Missing middle
Friendly frontage
Historic density

Image 12
Communal space
Integrated retail

Image 13
Green density
Missing middle
Friendly frontage
Photo credit: Elena Elisseeva/
Shutterstock

Image 14
Integrated transit
Photo credit: Wikimedia Commons

Image 15
Communal space

Image 16
Green density
Missing middle
Integrated transit
Integrated retail
Historic density
Photo credit: Ted Eytan/ Flickr

Image 17
Communal space
Integrated retail

Image 18
Green density
Missing middle
Communal space
Friendly frontage
Historic density
Photo credit: missingmiddlehousing.
com

Image 19:
Green density
Communal space

Image 20
Green density
Missing middle
Friendly frontage
Communal space
Photo credit: tacomahousing.org

Image 21
Green density
Communal space
Integrated retail

Image 22
Missing middle
Integrated retail
Historic density
Photo credit: Daniel Case/
Wikimedia

Image 23
Green density
Missing middle
Integrated transit
Friendly frontage
Photo credit: tacomahousing.org

Image 24
Green density
Missing middle
Communal space
Friendly frontage
Photo credit: seattle djc.com

Figure 5.3 Density survey images and density preference dimensions presented in each image.

Table 5.2 summarizes respondent living environments. Most respondents (54%) lived in a single-family house at the time, but a wide majority (84%) had previously lived in multi-family housing. Additionally, all respondents reported having at least some multi-family housing in their current neighborhood, ranging from a few types to many. Respondents also reported living in relatively well-serviced neighborhoods: generally, 80% or more reported having stores or transit, parks or playgrounds, and sidewalks or bike lanes nearby. Neighborhoods were also viewed by our

Table 5.2 Living environment characteristics

Living environment characteristics	%
Current housing type	
Single-family detached	54
Apartment/condo	31
Townhouse/rowhouse	8
Mixed-use building	4
Mobile home	3
Other	1
Previous housing	
Apartment/condo	84
Never in multi-family	16
Multi-family in current neighborhood?	
One or two types	36
Several types	34
Many types	30
Stores or transit nearby?	
Yes	78
No	22
Parks or playgrounds nearby?	
Yes	84
No	16
Sidewalks or bike lanes?	
Yes	81
No	19
Safe neighborhood?	
Yes	83
No	17
Current neighborhood	
Downtown	10
Suburban with shops	35
Suburban with houses only	17
Urban residential	24
Small town	8
Rural	6

respondents as overwhelmingly safe (83%). Participants reported living in a fairly wide variety of neighborhood types, ranging from suburban with shops (35%) to urban residential (24%) to downtowns (10%). Only 17% of respondents reported living in suburban areas with houses only.

Table 5.3 summarizes the individual characteristics of respondents. About half were female (53%), with the other half split between male (41%) and non-binary (6%). Most respondents (47%) were aged in their thirties or forties, were single (54%), and did not have children (71%); and most were either renters or living with family or friends (69%).

A clear majority of our participants had at least some college education or had a college degree. Income categories were fairly evenly split among three categories: low, middle, and high income. Our respondents were mostly White (61%) and non-Hispanic (88%), although a third of our respondents were non-White (Black or Asian).

Density preferences

Table 5.4 lists the images that were most liked in order from "somewhat agree" and "agree" to "somewhat disagree" and "disagree"—the least liked. The top third tier of eight images included dimensions of "green density" and "missing middle," and seven out of eight images also included "friendly frontage." Three out of eight in the top tier included communal space or historic density, while only 1 image included transit and retail.

In the middle tier, images again had some green density (5 out of 8 images), but there was less "missing middle" (3 out of 8). Communal space was slightly more prevalent (4 out of 8 images), while transit and "friendly frontage" were not dominant (2 out of 8). The least liked images (bottom third) had little green density. Two of the images in the bottom tier, liked by only 30% of respondents, possessed only transit as a characteristic dimension.

Finally, we looked at the differences between image preference and individual and living environment characteristics. For all respondents, we looked at three images in the top tier and three images in the bottom tier, using cross-tabulation tables to show the frequency distribution of variables and to point to possible correlations in the data.

In the top tier, image 13 had the strongest rating, with a combined agreement of 80%. Image 13, which contained the qualities of green density, missing middle, and friendly frontage, showed a modern residential neighborhood featuring a row of contemporary townhouses or low-rise apartment buildings. The buildings had a clean, modern design with brick facades and large windows, and each unit had a balcony with glass railings. Balconies, sidewalks, and planting areas were well-kept, with green lawns and trees lining the street. The landscaping was neat and orderly.

The second highest rating was for image 8, which had the added dimension of communal space (in addition to green density, missing middle,

Table 5.3 Individual characteristics

Individual characteristics	%
Gender	
Man	41
Woman	53
Non-Binary	6
Age	
Under 30	41
30s–40s	47
50+	12
Tenure	
Rent	43
Own	31
Living with family or friends	26
Children	
Yes	29
No	71
Marital status	
Single	54
Married	30
Living with partner(s)	16
Education	
High school	13
Some college	31
College grad	45
Post-grad	11
Income	
Under 50K	33
Middle Inc	39
100K+	27
Ethnicity	
Not Hispanic	88
Hispanic	12
Race	
White	61
Black or African American	19
Asian	16
Other	3

and friendly frontage). The image showed a row of traditionally styled, colorful townhouses in an all-residential environment. Each townhouse had a small front yard with well-maintained landscaping. The architectural style had a vintage feel, with gables, widely trimmed windows, and overhangs. Walkways ran between the homes, and black wrought iron fences lined the small front yards. The overall atmosphere was welcoming.

Another image in the top tier was image 16 that included a broader range of dimensions, including transit, retail, and historic components. The image depicted an urban street scene lined with buildings on both sides, featuring a mix of historic and modern architecture. The scene was fairly diverse, including a prominent brick, vintage building with a turret roof alongside more modern buildings. The public realm was prominent as well, with trees lining the sidewalk and a street that was well-maintained with clear pedestrian crosswalks. The overall scene conveyed a lively, well-developed urban neighborhood.

Image 5, one of the few images with a single dimension—transit—was in the bottom tier. The image showed a modern urban setting with a mix of residential and commercial buildings. Prominent in the image were boxy, contemporary apartment buildings typical of standard urban infill development. In the foreground, a light rail train was visible, indicating a well-developed public transportation system. The scene suggested a transit-oriented development with a somewhat corporate feel.

Another low-ranked image was image 7, ranked low despite having the qualities of green density, missing middle, and friendly frontage. The image showed a row of modern townhouses built in a contemporary architectural style with bold, colorful exteriors—a mix of blue, green, and orange facades. The style was decidedly modern with flat roofs and clean geometric lines. Each townhouse had a small front yard and steps leading up to a slightly elevated street-level entrance. The street itself was lined with bare trees (indicating a winter scene).

Finally, image 22 was low ranked and had the qualities of missing middle, integrated retail, and historic density. The image showed a classic small-town main street in the U.S. lined with historic buildings containing various businesses. The architecture was a stylistic mix, predominantly from the late 19th to early 20th centuries with brick facades, large windows, and decorative cornices. Cars were parked along the street with a few pedestrians visible. The presence of flags and banners indicated there was an organized effort to create a lively environment.

We next performed cross-tabulations for the three top and bottom-tier images described above. The six images were cross-tabbed with two living environmental characteristics (current housing and current neighborhood) and six individual characteristics (gender, age, tenure, education, income, and race). Tables A.1—A.3 list percentages for the top tier images, and Tables A.4–A.6 list the percentages for the bottom tier images.

Table 5.4 Density preferences and dimensions presented in each density examples

Tier	Images	Preference agreement							Density features presented in each image						
		Disagree	Somewhat disagree	Disagree/ Somewhat disagree	Neither agree/ disagree	Somewhat agree	Agree	Somewhat agree/Agree	GREEN	MIDDLE	COMMUNAL	TRANSIT	FRIENDLY	RETAIL	HISTORIC
	Image 13	6%	8%	**14%**	6%	42%	38%	**80%**	*	*			*		
	Image 8	4%	10%	**14%**	13%	37%	36%	**73%**	*	*	*		*		
	Image 24	7%	10%	**17%**	12%	34%	37%	**71%**	*	*	*		*		
	Image 1	9%	13%	**22%**	10%	41%	26%	**67%**	*	*			*		
Top	Image 11	11%	11%	**22%**	13%	43%	22%	**65%**	*	*			*		*
	Image 20	9%	19%	**28%**	11%	41%	20%	**61%**	*	*	*		*		
	Image 16	10%	16%	**26%**	13%	35%	25%	**60%**	*	*		*		*	*
	Image 4	12%	19%	**31%**	10%	37%	22%	**59%**	*	*			*		*

Image 18	12%	19%	**31%**	12%	37%	20%	**57%**
Image 21	13%	19%	**32%**	14%	33%	20%	**53%**
Image 23	16%	23%	**39%**	12%	33%	17%	**50%**
Image 17	19%	22%	**41%**	13%	33%	13%	**46%**
Middle — Image 2	25%	21%	**46%**	8%	35%	11%	**46%**
Image 15	22%	19%	**41%**	13%	28%	17%	**45%**
Image 3	27%	23%	**50%**	6%	33%	11%	**44%**
Image 6	19%	23%	**42%**	13%	35%	9%	**44%**

(Continued)

Table 5.4 (Continued)

Tier	Images	Preference agreement							Density features presented in each image						
		Disagree	Somewhat disagree	Somewhat disagree/ Disagree	Neither agree/ disagree	Somewhat agree	Agree	Somewhat agree/Agree	GREEN	MIDDLE	COMMUNAL	TRANSIT	FRIENDLY	RETAIL	HISTORIC
	Image 19	24%	25%	**49%**	10%	31%	10%	**41%**	*		*				
	Image 7	19%	26%	**45%**	16%	25%	15%	**40%**	*	*			*		
	Image 12	25%	25%	**50%**	12%	28%	10%	**38%**			*			*	
	Image 10	27%	28%	**55%**	10%	26%	9%	**35%**		*				*	*
Bottom	Image 14	35%	24%	**59%**	10%	23%	9%	**32%**				*			
	Image 22	29%	28%	**57%**	12%	21%	10%	**31%**		*				*	*
	Image 5	35%	27%	**62%**	8%	24%	6%	**30%**				*			
	Image 9	33%	32%	**65%**	12%	18%	5%	**23%**		*					*

For the highly ranked image 13 (Table A.1), all housing types prompted positive agreement, although those living in single-family housing assigned slightly lower ratings. Mixed-use and townhouse/rowhouse residents were assigned the highest. Rural residents produced the least favorable responses, followed by small-town residents; however, downtown respondents produced the highest. There were no clear gender or educational differences, but younger groups responded more favorably than older groups, and Asian groups generated slightly more favorable responses than White groups.

Image 8 (Table A.2) again showed the strongest agreement for mixed-use and townhouse/rowhouse residents, and the least agreement for single-family detached dwellers (although still overall positive). There was strong preference from downtown respondents, and less from a small town and rural residents. Older respondents were three times more likely to respond less favorably than respondents under age 30. Women, renters, and middle-income respondents gave the most favorable responses. There were no pronounced racial differences noted.

For image 16 (Table A.3), a more complex and urban image, disagreement was highest among single-family housing and rural respondents. Downtown respondents gave the most favorable responses (50% "strongly agree"). Gender differences were minimal, but younger respondents produced more favorable responses than those who were older. Those with a high-school education gave much higher "neutral" ratings for this image than other groups.

Which respondents found something positive among the bottom tier of images? Respondents were split in their responses to image 5 that showed prominent light rail and mid-level high-rises. While downtown respondents predominantly liked the image (56% agreed), 39% did not. Suburban residents were mostly negative in their responses, although a third of the residents in "suburban with houses only" environments produced positive responses. There were some differences in terms of individual characteristics: men under 30 and those with more education gave more favorable responses. Racially, Asians produced the most favorable responses, while Black and White respondents were aligned in their preferences (Table A.4).

Respondent impressions of image 7, with its colorful, modern architecture, were also somewhat bifurcated—some agreeing, some disagreeing—but the most negative views were from residents of single-family housing. However, in all cases, a third or more of the respondents agreed that the image was a place they would like to live. Renters and younger residents (under 30) offered more favorable responses (Table A.5).

Finally, image 22, a traditional main street, generated the lowest ratings among townhouse/rowhouse dwellers (73% disagreed). On the other hand, although there were negative ratings across the board, a third of downtown, urban residential, suburban with houses only, and small-town respondents had positive views about living on a main street. Men and older respondents were somewhat more receptive to this image, but the ratings were fairly consistent across tenure, education, income, and race (Table A.6).

We investigated the differences between image ratings for different living environments closely. We compared three groups: those living in downtown or urban residential (63 respondents or 34% of our survey), those living in suburban areas (97 respondents or 52% of our survey), and those in rural or small-town areas (26 of respondents or 14% of our survey).

Overall, and perhaps not surprisingly, downtown/urban residential residents produced the most favorable responses. For 14 out of the 24 images, at least 50% of the respondents rated the images as either "somewhat agree" or "strongly agree." This number dropped to 11 out of 24 images for suburban respondents, and further dropped to only five images for rural/small-town respondents. Low favorability was reflected similarly. Only 3 out of 24 images had an above-50% disagreement rating among downtown dwellers, while suburban respondents produced above 50% disagreement on eight images, and rural/small-town respondents produced above 50% disagreement on 13 density images.

Referring to Figure 5.4, images 1, 11, 13, 16, and 24 were ranked the highest by rural and small-town participants (more than half agreed or strongly agreed that it was a place they would like to live). All of the images in this group contained dimensions of "green density," "missing middle," and all but one also contained "friendly frontage." At least half of the participants in rural and small-towns ranked images 14 and 19 as "strongly disagree" when asked if they would like to live there (Figure 5.5). These images were of urban environments with mid-rise apartment buildings and light rail trains prominently visible, and revealed a strong emphasis on public transportation and a somewhat corporate-looking, boxy density.

Suburban respondents responded most favorably to images 8, 13, and 24—all of which contained dimensions of green density in the absence of middle and friendly frontage; two of the three also showed communal space. All three images depicted townhouse or rowhouse density form, with residential housing as a series of connected homes with shared walls. The overall appearance of all three images was of a well-maintained area with landscaping and street trees. There was also a strong focus on curb appeal with neat facades and attractive entryways. Suburban respondents reacted least favorably to images 5 and 14, although only a minority (37% and 39%, respectively) were in the "strongly disagree" category.

Like suburban respondents, downtown/urban residential respondents rated images 8 and 13 very highly, with 86% and 81% agreement, respectively. Unlike suburban respondents, image 24 was not as highly ranked. In terms of disagreement, downtown/urban residential residents generated the lowest favorability ratings for images 5 and 22, with "strongly disagree" ratings for 32% of respondents. On the other hand, these two images had higher percentages (40% and 37%, respectively) of respondents rating them "somewhat agree" or "strongly agree."

Figures 5.4 and 5.5 summarize these differences graphically. Overall, there was more agreement between the two downtown/urban

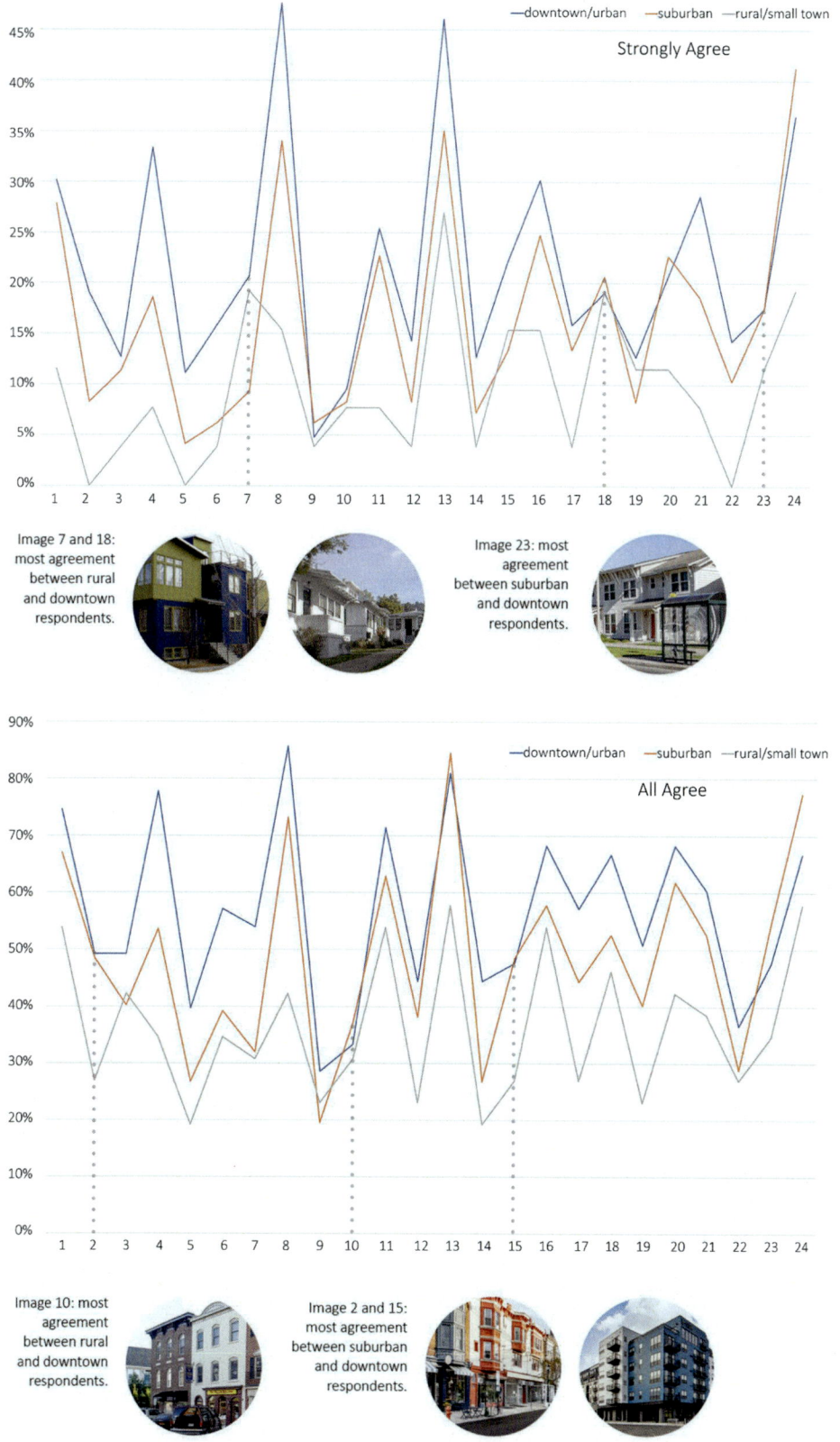

Figure 5.4 Density image agreement among downtown, suburban and rural/small town respondents.

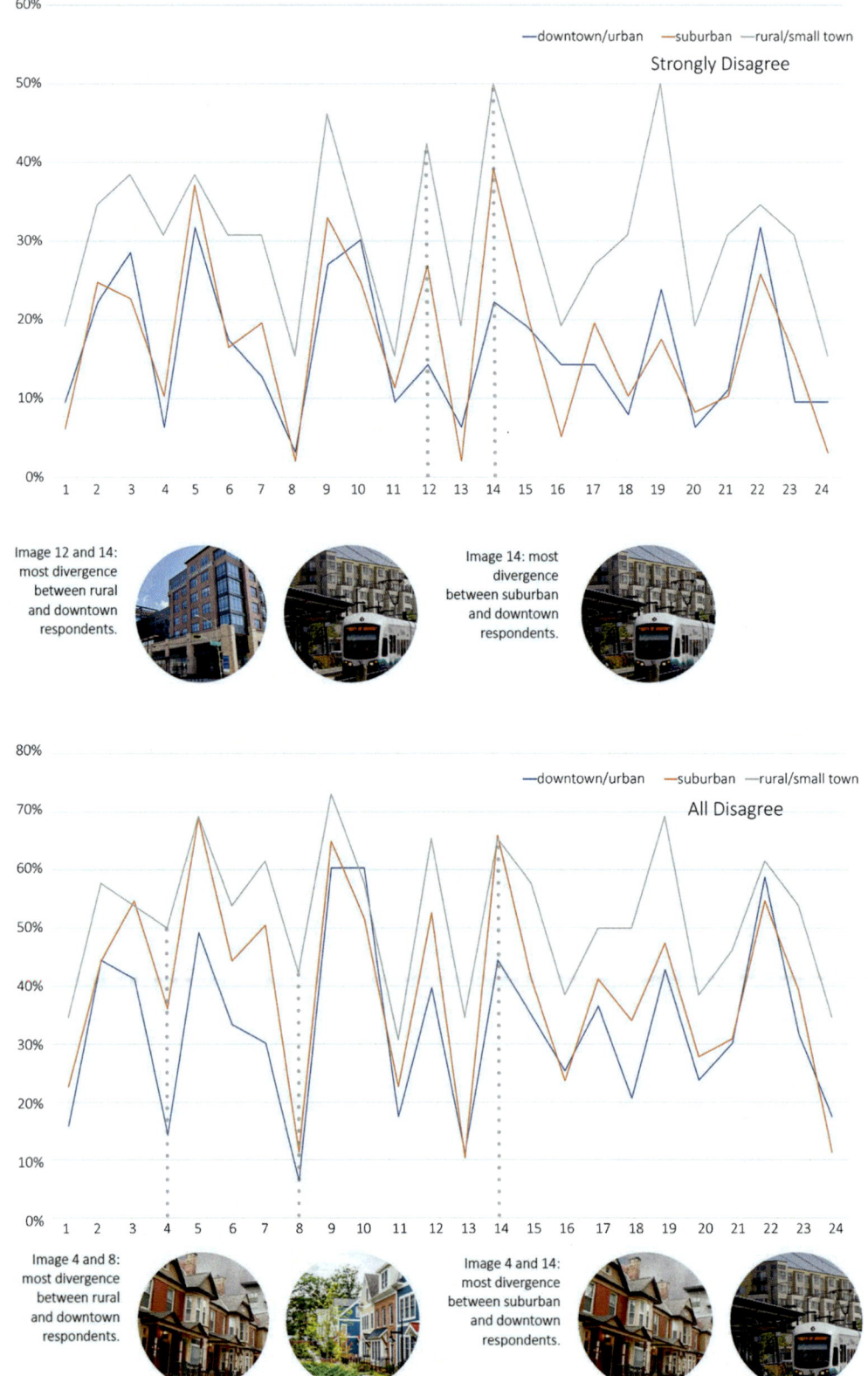

Figure 5.5 Density image disagreement among downtown, suburban and rural/small town respondents.

residential and suburban groups, and the most disagreement between downtown/urban residential and rural/small-town respondents. But there were interesting exceptions. As Figure 5.4 shows, the strongest alignment between downtown and rural voters in terms of the agreement was on images 7 and 18—one in five respondents in both groups said they "strongly agreed" that these were places they would like to live. This is particularly interesting since overall, image 7 was situated in the bottom tier (Table 5.4). When "strongly agree" and "somewhat agree" were combined ("All Agree" in Figure 5.4), the most agreement between rural and downtown voters was for image 10, with one-third of respondents in both groups marking the agreement. The image was of a mixed-use, traditional main street with housing above storefronts. Figure 5.4 also shows that downtown and suburban respondents were fairly well aligned, with images 2, 15, and 23 having the most agreement. In the total ranking (Table 5.4), these images all fell into the middle tier.

The most divergence between downtown and rural voters in terms of strong disagreement was for images 12 and 14, as shown in Figure 5.5. Both images showed fairly urban and dense mid-rise developments, with little to no green (image 14 was dominated by light rail). Image 14 was divergent in three aspects—a relatively high difference in rating between rural and downtown respondents, and between suburban and downtown respondents measured both ways (strong disagreement and all disagreement). When both "somewhat disagree" and "strongly disagree" were combined (all disagreement), the greatest difference was with images 4 and 8, two images with traditional architectural style in rowhouse form. However, overall, both images were highly rated and in the top tier.

Conclusion

Our survey was designed to better understand the qualities of density that might make it more acceptable and even preferred. We did not show images of single-family homes versus high-rises which would have surveyed contrasting density extremes. Instead, our images varied by dimensions that might accompany density green, missing middle, communal space, friendly frontage, transit, retail, and historic architecture.

The current housing and living environment did seem to matter. Those currently living in single-family detached housing or in small towns and rural areas were the least positive about density overall. On the other hand, there was a somewhat surprising level of agreement between suburban and downtown or urban residential respondents—rural/small-town resident responses showed more divergence.

However, rural and small-town respondents did find some dimensions of density to like. A majority agreed that a selection of images were in fact places they would like to live—in addition to green space and missing middle housing, images characterized by historic architecture (images 11 and 16) and communal space or friendly frontages (images 1, 13, and 24).

Since these respondents leaned less favorably toward density overall, this finding sends the message that it is indeed possible to find ways to build densely in ways that even the toughest density critics, or those least familiar with it, might find appealing.

Individual characteristics pointed to a few interesting preference variations. Asian respondents often had more positive views of density than Black and White respondents. Those with more education seemed to respond more positively to density, while those with no more than a high-school education often responded with less positive agreement. Consistent with the literature on density, there tended to be more support for density among renters and younger people. As discussed in the introduction, this suggests that overall population acceptance may increase over time as renting becomes a more common and even preferred option, and as younger generations who are more open to density replace older generations who find it less acceptable.

It is not particularly surprising that images showing "green density," "missing middle" and "friendly frontage" were so highly rated. Somewhat more surprising was that transit and retail options were not rated higher, perhaps because of image quality. A train or bus running through a neighborhood may not be the best way to communicate the value of transit access. Still, the low ranking by a broad swath of respondents for image 5 (showing a prominent light rail and mid-level high-rises) is a cautionary tale, since so much of American infill development tends to look like the image shown—stripped-down, corporate-looking architecture. While there was one tree shown in image 5, the image lacked what was consistently most liked by participants: greenery, missing middle housing, communal elements, and friendly frontage.

Our survey pointed to a certain fluidity of density preferences. We found that images could have the qualities of green density, missing middle, and friendly frontage, but still be low ranked (image 7, for example), but we also found that even with some of the lowest rated images, one-third or more of the respondents often viewed them positively. There is hope, then, that if density is designed in appealing ways—making it more desirable—the benefits of density might become attainable. Thus, two main conclusions are warranted: multiple density options are needed, and "the devil is in the details."

Note

1   The participants were recruited through a volunteer-based website (Prolific.com) and paid $20 USD when successfully completing the survey. This study was approved by the Institutional Review Board (IRB) of the University of Minnesota (IRB ID: STUDY00021607).

Literature cited

Andrews, F. J., & Warner, E. (2020). 'Living outside the house': How families raising young children in new, private high-rise developments experience their local environment. *Journal of Urbanism: International Research on Placemaking and Urban Sustainability*, *13*(3), 263–285.

Azizi, M. M. (2020). Challenges of density increase and carrying capacity in established urban neighborhoods: Empirical experiences. *Journal of Urban Planning and Development*, *146*(4), 04020040. https://doi.org/10.1061/(asce)up.1943-5444.0000617.

Billig, N. S., Smith, C. A., & Moyer, R. (2020). Residents' preferences for private amenities and trade-offs associated with various spatial densities and patterns. *Journal of Urbanism: International Research on Placemaking and Urban Sustainability*, *13*(3), 286–302. https://doi.org/10.1080/17549175.2020.1726796.

Bolleter, J., Myers, Z., & Hooper, P. (2021). Delivering medium-density infill development through promoting the benefits and limiting background infill. *Journal of Urban Design*, *26*(4), 441–466. https://doi.org/10.1080/13574809.2020.1854610.

Brain, D. (2005). From good neighborhoods to sustainable cities: Social science and the social agenda of the new urbanism. *International Regional Science Review*, *28*(2), 217–238.

Calthorpe, P. (1993). The *next American metropolis: Ecology, community, and the American dream* (Vol. 23). New York: Princeton Architectural Press.

Campoli, J. (2012). *Made for walking: Density and neighborhood form*. Cambridge, MA: Lincoln Institute of Land Policy.

Campoli, J., & Maclean, A. (2007). *Visualizing density*. Cambridge: Lincoln Institute of Land Policy.

Condon, P. M. (2020). *Five rules for tomorrow's cities: Design in an age of urban migration, demographic change, and a disappearing middle class*. Illustrated edition. Washington, DC, Covelo, CA, London: Island Press.

Davis, J., Rong, H., & Huennekens, J. W. (2023). Perceptions toward upzoning: A parcel-level analysis of public sentiments toward the Minneapolis 2040 plan. *Journal of Planning Education and Research*. https://doi.org/10.1177/0739456X231205584.

Degen, M. M., & Rose, G. (2012). The sensory experiencing of urban design: The role of walking and perceptual memory. *Urban Studies*, *49*(15), 3271–3287. https://doi.org/10.1177/0042098012440463.

Ehrenhalt, A. (2019). 'Vertical villages' may be the future of urban living. That's scary. *Governing*. March 19, 2019. https://www.governing.com/archive/gov-vertical-villages.html.

Fischel, W. A. (2005). *The homevoter hypothesis: How home values influence local government taxation, school finance, and land-use policies*. Cambridge, MA: Harvard University Press.

Hankinson, M. (2018). When do renters behave like homeowners? High rent, price anxiety, and NIMBYism. *American Political Science Review*, *112*(3), 473–493. https://doi.org/10.1017/S0003055418000035.

Jacobs, J. (1961). *The death and life of great American cities*. New York: Vintage Books.

Karimi, A., Delavar, M. R., Mohammadi, M., & Ghadirian, P. (2020). Spatial urban density modelling using the concept of carrying capacity: A case study of Isfahan, Iran. *Journal of Urbanism: International Research on Placemaking and Urban Sustainability*, *13*(4), 489–512. https://doi.org/10.1080/17549175.2020.1753225.

Krier, L. (2009). *The architecture of community*. Washington, DC: Island Press.

Kyttä, M., Kahila, M., & Broberg, A. (2011). Perceived environmental quality as an input to urban infill policy-making. *Urban Design International*, *16*, 19–35. https://doi.org/10.1057/udi.2010.19.

Manville, M., Monkkonen, P., & Lens, M. (2020). It's time to end single-family zoning. *Journal of the American Planning Association*, *86*(1), 106–112.

Mouratidis, K., & Andersen, B. (2023). What makes people stay longer in the densifying city? Exploring the neighbourhood environment and social ties. *Housing Studies*, 1–22. https://doi.org/10.1080/02673037.2023.2185593.

Mousavinia, S. F., Pourdeihimi, S., & Madani, R. (2019). Housing layout, perceived density and social interactions in gated communities: Mediational role of territoriality. *Sustainable Cities and Society*, *51*, 101699. https://doi.org/10.1016/j.scs.2019.101699.

Navarrete-Hernandez, P., Mace, A., Karlsson, J., Holman, N., & Zorloni, D. A. (2022). Delivering higher density suburban development: The impact of building design and residents' attitudes. *Urban Studies*, *59*(13), 2801–2820. https://doi.org/10.1177/00420980211036633.

Nematollahi, S., Tiwari, R., & Hedgecock, D. (2016). Desirable dense neighbourhoods: An environmental psychological approach for understanding community resistance to densification. *Urban Policy and Research*, *34*(2), 132–151. https://doi.org/10.1080/08111146.2015.1078233.

Opit, S., Witten, K., & Kearns, R. (2020). Housing pathways, aspirations and preferences of young adults within increasing urban density. *Housing Studies*, *35*(1), 123–142. https://doi.org/10.1080/02673037.2019.1584662.

Park, K., Ewing, R., Sabouri, S., & Larsen, J. (2019). Street life and the built environment in an auto-oriented US region. *Cities*, *88*, 243–251. https://doi.org/10.1016/j.cities.2018.11.005.

Parolek, D. G. (2020). *Missing middle housing: Thinking big and building small to respond to today's housing crisis*. Washington, DC: Island Press.

Pfeiffer, D., Pearthree, G., & Ehlenz, M. M. (2019). Inventing what millennials want downtown: Housing the urban generation in low-density metropolitan regions. *Journal of Urbanism: International Research on Placemaking and Urban Sustainability*, *12*(4), 433–455. https://doi.org/10.1080/17549175.2019.1626267.

Price, A. (2018). Surprising approaches to achieving density. *Strong Towns Journal*. https://www.strongtowns.org/journal/2018/1/3/comparing-approaches-to-achieving-density (accessed June 2, 2022).

Sivam, A., Karuppannan, S., & Davis, M. C. (2012). Stakeholders' perception of residential density: A case study of Adelaide, Australia. *Journal of Housing and the Built Environment*, *27*, 473–494. https://doi.org/10.1007/s10901-011-9265-2.

Sotoudeh, H., & Abdullah, W. M. Z. W. (2013). Evaluation of fitness of design in urban historical context: From the perspectives of residents. *Frontiers of Architectural Research*, *2*(1), 85–93. https://doi.org/10.1016/j.foar.2012.10.007

Talen, E., & Wileden, L. (2024). The density puzzle: What is known, what is disputed, and where to go from here. *Journal of Planning Literature*, 08854122241262750.

Thomas, L. L. (2020). Committed and "won over" parents in Vancouver's dense family-oriented urbanism. *Journal of the American Planning Association*, *87*(2), 239–253. https://doi.org/10.1080/01944363.2020.1834871.

Trounstine, J. (2023). You won't be my neighbor: Opposition to high density development. *Urban Affairs Review*, *59*(1), 294–308. https://doi.org/10.1177/10780874211065776.

Whittemore, A. H., & BenDor, T. K. (2019). Opposition to housing development in a suburban US County: Characteristics, origins, and consequences. *Land Use Policy*, *88*, 104158. https://doi.org/10.1016/j.landusepol.2019.104158.

Wicki, M., Kauer, F., Hofer, K., & Kaufmann, D. (2022, September). The politics of densification: Who wants to regulate housing development how? In *118th American Political Science Association Annual Meeting and Exhibition (APSA 2022)*. ETH Zurich, Institute for Spatial and Landscape Development. https://doi.org/10.3929/ETHZ-B-000570236.

Yanarella, E. J., & Levine, R. S. (2011). The sustainable cities manifesto. In *The city as fulcrum of global sustainability* (pp. 23–40). Anthem Press. https://doi.org/10.7135/UPO9780857284006.004.

APPENDIX A

Table A.1 Cross-tabulation for Image 13

Current housing		Apartment/ Condo	Mixed-use	Single-family detached	Townhouse/ Rowhouse		
	Strongly disagree	0%	0%	8%	0%		
	Somewhat disagree	5%	0%	10%	7%		
	Neutral	4%	14%	7%	13%		
	Somewhat agree	47%	29%	42%	27%		
	Strongly agree	44%	57%	33%	53%		

Current Neighborhood		Downtown	Urban residential	Suburban with shops	Suburban with houses only	Small town	Rural
	Strongly disagree	6%	7%	3%	0%	14%	25%
	Somewhat disagree	6%	4%	6%	13%	14%	17%
	Neutral	0%	11%	5%	6%	7%	8%
	Somewhat agree	44%	31%	55%	38%	36%	25%
	Strongly agree	44%	47%	31%	44%	29%	25%

Gender		Man	Non-binary	Woman			
	Strongly disagree	5%	0%	7%			
	Somewhat disagree	5%	25%	8%			
	Neutral	9%	0%	5%			
	Somewhat agree	42%	17%	45%			
	Strongly agree	38%	58%	35%			

Age		Under 30	30s-40s	50+			
	Strongly disagree	3%	6%	18%			
	Somewhat disagree	6%	9%	9%			

(Continued)

Table A.1 (Continued)

Age		Under 30	30s-40s	50+	
	Neutral	3%	8%	14%	
	Somewhat agree	44%	43%	32%	
	Strongly agree	44%	34%	27%	
Tenure		Living with family/friends	Own	Rent	
	Strongly disagree	2%	14%	3%	
	Somewhat disagree	8%	10%	6%	
	Neutral	2%	16%	3%	
	Somewhat agree	46%	34%	45%	
	Strongly agree	42%	26%	44%	
Education		High school	Some college	College grad	Post-grad
	Strongly disagree	0%	7%	7%	5%
	Somewhat disagree	12%	5%	8%	10%
	Neutral	4%	9%	6%	5%
	Somewhat agree	52%	29%	45%	55%
	Strongly agree	32%	50%	34%	25%
Income		Under 50K	Middle income	100K+	
	Strongly disagree	7%	6%	6%	
	Somewhat disagree	8%	10%	6%	
	Neutral	7%	3%	12%	
	Somewhat agree	44%	35%	48%	
	Strongly agree	34%	47%	28%	
Race		Asian	Black	White	
	Strongly disagree	0%	3%	9%	
	Somewhat disagree	7%	8%	9%	
	Neutral	10%	11%	4%	
	Somewhat agree	33%	31%	46%	
	Strongly agree	50%	47%	32%	

Table A.2 Cross-tabulation for Image 8

Current housing		Apartment/ Condo	Mixed-use	Single-family detached	Townhouse/ Rowhouse		
	Strongly disagree	0%	0%	6%	0%		
	Somewhat disagree	7%	0%	11%	7%		
	Neutral	14%	14%	14%	7%		
	Somewhat agree	39%	57%	33%	47%		
	Strongly agree	40%	29%	36%	40%		

Current Neighborhood		Downtown	Urban residential	Suburban with shops	Suburban with houses only	Small town	Rural
	Strongly disagree	0%	4%	0%	6%	14%	17%
	Somewhat disagree	0%	4%	9%	9%	29%	25%
	Neutral	6%	9%	14%	19%	21%	8%
	Somewhat agree	50%	33%	37%	44%	21%	33%
	Strongly agree	44%	49%	40%	22%	14%	17%

Gender		Man	Non-binary	Woman			
	Strongly disagree	4%	8%	4%			
	Somewhat disagree	12%	8%	8%			
	Neutral	18%	8%	9%			
	Somewhat agree	37%	42%	37%			
	Strongly agree	29%	33%	42%			

Age		Under 30	30s-40s	50+			
	Strongly disagree	3%	5%	9%			
	Somewhat disagree	8%	8%	23%			
	Neutral	12%	11%	23%			
	Somewhat agree	34%	40%	36%			
	Strongly agree	44%	36%	9%			

(Continued)

Table A.2 (Continued)

Tenure		Living with family/friends	Own	Rent	
	Strongly disagree	4%	9%	1%	
	Somewhat disagree	6%	10%	11%	
	Neutral	17%	14%	10%	
	Somewhat agree	38%	38%	36%	
	Strongly agree	35%	29%	41%	
Education		High school	Some college	College grad	Post-grad
	Strongly disagree	0%	7%	5%	0%
	Somewhat disagree	16%	9%	8%	10%
	Neutral	12%	12%	16%	5%
	Somewhat agree	44%	28%	39%	50%
	Strongly agree	28%	45%	33%	35%
Income		Under 50K	Middle income	100K+	
	Strongly disagree	7%	4%	2%	
	Somewhat disagree	13%	6%	12%	
	Neutral	13%	11%	14%	
	Somewhat agree	43%	25%	48%	
	Strongly agree	25%	54%	24%	
Race		Asian	Black	White	
	Strongly disagree	0%	11%	4%	
	Somewhat disagree	13%	6%	11%	
	Neutral	13%	14%	11%	
	Somewhat agree	50%	28%	36%	
	Strongly agree	23%	42%	39%	

Table A.3 Cross-tabulation for Image 16

Current housing		Apartment/ Condo	Mixed-use	Single-family detached	Townhouse/ Rowhouse		
	Strongly disagree	5%	0%	13%	7%		
	Somewhat disagree	18%	0%	15%	13%		
	Neutral	16%	0%	11%	20%		
	Somewhat agree	37%	71%	35%	33%		
	Strongly agree	25%	29%	26%	27%		
Current Neighborhood		Downtown	Urban residential	Suburban with shops	Suburban with houses only	Small town	Rural
	Strongly disagree	11%	16%	6%	3%	7%	33%
	Somewhat disagree	6%	13%	22%	13%	21%	17%
	Neutral	0%	9%	17%	22%	7%	8%
	Somewhat agree	33%	40%	32%	34%	50%	25%
	Strongly agree	50%	22%	23%	28%	14%	17%
Gender		Man	Non-binary	Woman			
	Strongly disagree	7%	8%	13%			
	Somewhat disagree	21%	8%	13%			
	Neutral	14%	8%	12%			
	Somewhat agree	33%	58%	35%			
	Strongly agree	25%	17%	27%			
Age		Under 30	30s-40s	50+			
	Strongly disagree	10%	8%	18%			
	Somewhat disagree	17%	16%	14%			
	Neutral	12%	10%	27%			
	Somewhat agree	39%	37%	18%			
	Strongly agree	22%	29%	23%			

(Continued)

Table A.3 (Continued)

Tenure		Living with family/ friends	Own	Rent	
	Strongly disagree	10%	14%	8%	
	Somewhat disagree	15%	21%	14%	
	Neutral	15%	14%	11%	
	Somewhat agree	35%	28%	41%	
	Strongly agree	25%	24%	26%	
Education		High school	Some college	College grad	Post-grad
	Strongly disagree	12%	12%	11%	0%
	Somewhat disagree	16%	12%	18%	20%
	Neutral	32%	10%	8%	15%
	Somewhat agree	20%	40%	39%	30%
	Strongly agree	20%	26%	24%	35%
Income		Under 50K	Middle income	100K+	
	Strongly disagree	10%	13%	8%	
	Somewhat disagree	15%	15%	20%	
	Neutral	16%	13%	10%	
	Somewhat agree	38%	29%	38%	
	Strongly agree	21%	31%	24%	
Race		Asian	Black	White	
	Strongly disagree	3%	17%	11%	
	Somewhat disagree	27%	19%	13%	
	Neutral	7%	17%	13%	
	Somewhat agree	50%	22%	35%	
	Strongly agree	13%	25%	28%	

Table A.4 Cross-tabulation for Image 5

Current housing		Apartment/ Condo	Mixed-use	Single-family detached	Townhouse/ Rowhouse		
	Strongly disagree	23%	0%	43%	47%		
	Somewhat disagree	33%	14%	24%	13%		
	Neutral	14%	14%	4%	7%		
	Somewhat agree	21%	43%	25%	33%		
	Strongly agree	9%	29%	4%	0%		

Current Neighborhood		Downtown	Urban residential	Suburban with shops	Suburban with houses only	Small town	Rural
	Strongly disagree	11%	40%	35%	41%	36%	42%
	Somewhat disagree	28%	13%	37%	22%	21%	42%
	Neutral	6%	13%	5%	3%	14%	8%
	Somewhat agree	39%	24%	18%	31%	29%	8%
	Strongly agree	17%	9%	5%	3%	0%	0%

Gender		Man	Non-binary	Woman
	Strongly disagree	32%	33%	39%
	Somewhat disagree	21%	33%	31%
	Neutral	9%	8%	6%
	Somewhat agree	34%	17%	17%
	Strongly agree	4%	8%	7%

Age		Under 30	30s-40s	50+
	Strongly disagree	36%	34%	36%
	Somewhat disagree	25%	25%	41%
	Neutral	5%	9%	9%
	Somewhat agree	25%	28%	9%
	Strongly agree	9%	3%	5%

(Continued)

Table A.4 (Continued)

Tenure		Living with family/ friends	Own	Rent	
	Strongly disagree	33%	40%	34%	
	Somewhat disagree	31%	24%	26%	
	Neutral	2%	12%	8%	
	Somewhat agree	31%	22%	21%	
	Strongly agree	2%	2%	11%	
Education		High school	Some college	College grad	Post-grad
	Strongly disagree	52%	29%	39%	20%
	Somewhat disagree	28%	29%	27%	20%
	Neutral	4%	7%	6%	20%
	Somewhat agree	16%	29%	22%	30%
	Strongly agree	0%	5%	7%	10%
Income		Under 50K	Middle income	100K+	
	Strongly disagree	34%	39%	32%	
	Somewhat disagree	36%	21%	24%	
	Neutral	5%	4%	16%	
	Somewhat agree	21%	24%	28%	
	Strongly agree	3%	13%	0%	
Race		Asian	Black	White	
	Strongly disagree	27%	36%	36%	
	Somewhat disagree	13%	28%	31%	
	Neutral	10%	6%	8%	
	Somewhat agree	40%	25%	20%	
	Strongly agree	10%	6%	5%	

Table A.5 Cross-tabulation for Image 7

Current housing		Apartment/ Condo	Mixed-use	Single-family detached	Townhouse/ Rowhouse		
	Strongly disagree	19%	0%	19%	7%		
	Somewhat disagree	19%	14%	30%	27%		
	Neutral	12%	29%	16%	27%		
	Somewhat agree	33%	43%	22%	13%		
	Strongly agree	16%	14%	13%	27%		
Current Neighborhood		Downtown	Urban residential	Suburban with shops	Suburban with houses only	Small town	Rural
	Strongly disagree	6%	16%	18%	22%	36%	25%
	Somewhat disagree	39%	9%	32%	28%	29%	33%
	Neutral	11%	18%	15%	22%	7%	8%
	Somewhat agree	28%	36%	23%	22%	14%	8%
	Strongly agree	17%	22%	11%	6%	14%	25%
Gender		Man	Non-binary	Woman			
	Strongly disagree	22%	8%	17%			
	Somewhat disagree	25%	17%	29%			
	Neutral	18%	25%	12%			
	Somewhat agree	25%	42%	22%			
	Strongly agree	9%	8%	19%			
Age		Under 30	30s–40s	50+			
	Strongly disagree	23%	14%	23%			
	Somewhat disagree	21%	29%	36%			
	Neutral	13%	17%	18%			
	Somewhat agree	27%	25%	14%			
	Strongly agree	16%	15%	9%			

(Continued)

Table A.5 (Continued)

Tenure		Living with family/friends	Own	Rent	
	Strongly disagree	27%	17%	15%	
	Somewhat disagree	23%	33%	24%	
	Neutral	13%	19%	15%	
	Somewhat agree	23%	21%	29%	
	Strongly agree	15%	10%	18%	

Education		High school	Some college	College grad	Post-grad
	Strongly disagree	32%	19%	18%	5%
	Somewhat disagree	16%	24%	29%	35%
	Neutral	28%	16%	12%	15%
	Somewhat agree	16%	24%	24%	40%
	Strongly agree	8%	17%	17%	5%

Income		Under 50K	Middle income	100K+	
	Strongly disagree	31%	15%	10%	
	Somewhat disagree	18%	21%	44%	
	Neutral	16%	13%	18%	
	Somewhat agree	26%	25%	24%	
	Strongly agree	8%	26%	4%	

Race		Asian	Black	White	
	Strongly disagree	7%	33%	18%	
	Somewhat disagree	43%	11%	26%	
	Neutral	13%	11%	18%	
	Somewhat agree	17%	28%	25%	
	Strongly agree	20%	17%	13%	

Table A.6 Cross-tabulation for Image 22

Current housing		Apartment/ Condo	Mixed-use	Single-family detached	Townhouse/ Rowhouse		
	Strongly disagree	25%	14%	29%	53%		
	Somewhat disagree	28%	14%	29%	20%		
	Neutral	12%	14%	12%	7%		
	Somewhat agree	21%	43%	22%	13%		
	Strongly agree	14%	14%	8%	7%		
Current Neighborhood		Downtown	Urban residential	Suburban with shops	Suburban with houses only	Small town	Rural
	Strongly disagree	22%	36%	26%	25%	29%	42%
	Somewhat disagree	28%	27%	32%	22%	29%	25%
	Neutral	6%	4%	15%	19%	7%	17%
	Somewhat agree	28%	20%	15%	25%	36%	17%
	Strongly agree	17%	13%	11%	9%	0%	0%
Gender		Man	Non-binary	Woman			
	Strongly disagree	25%	17%	34%			
	Somewhat disagree	28%	42%	27%			
	Neutral	14%	0%	11%			
	Somewhat agree	24%	25%	18%			
	Strongly agree	9%	17%	10%			
Age		Under 30	30s-40s	50+			
	Strongly disagree	30%	31%	18%			
	Somewhat disagree	34%	22%	32%			
	Neutral	10%	11%	18%			
	Somewhat agree	14%	26%	23%			
	Strongly agree	12%	9%	9%			

(Continued)

Table A.6 (Continued)

Tenure		Living with family/ friends	Own	Rent	
	Strongly disagree	31%	26%	30%	
	Somewhat disagree	27%	33%	25%	
	Neutral	13%	10%	13%	
	Somewhat agree	19%	24%	20%	
	Strongly agree	10%	7%	13%	
Education		High school	Some college	College grad	Post-grad
	Strongly disagree	20%	22%	36%	30%
	Somewhat disagree	40%	33%	19%	35%
	Neutral	16%	16%	10%	5%
	Somewhat agree	20%	21%	24%	10%
	Strongly agree	4%	9%	11%	20%
Income		Under 50K	Middle income	100K+	
	Strongly disagree	26%	38%	22%	
	Somewhat disagree	34%	18%	34%	
	Neutral	8%	13%	14%	
	Somewhat agree	25%	19%	18%	
	Strongly agree	7%	13%	12%	
Race		Asian	Black	White	
	Strongly disagree	27%	44%	26%	
	Somewhat disagree	30%	22%	30%	
	Neutral	20%	11%	10%	
	Somewhat agree	17%	11%	24%	
	Strongly agree	7%	11%	11%	

6

DENSITY STRATEGIES FOR LIVING CLOSER

Green density

The incorporation of street tree planning is one of the main strategies available for achieving green density. Such planning takes into consideration both natural and built street elements in an effort to improve pedestrians' public safety and experience. In addition to assuring responsible street tree maintenance, streetscape design strategies include measures for sidewalk improvements, adequate street lighting and seating, effective landscape design, and public transport stops. Successful streetscape design provides safety, comfort, and accessibility for all users.

Green density can be achieved by implementing relatively small design interventions into under-maintained and underutilized informal open spaces. Figure 6.1 illustrates how neglected surface parking areas can become multi-use, flexible community spaces, and how alleyways can serve as informal public spaces where community farming classes can be held and gardening plots can be rented to residents. Figure 6.1 is an example of Cluster 1 in Chicago that is mainly characterized by relatively high multi-family residential density and easily accessed transit and commercial buildings, but it lacks tree canopy density and sidewalk connectivity. Suggested green density interventions could enrich residential life by improving access to green amenities and promoting informal neighborhood activities.

Green density generates various environmental sustainability benefits, such as a smaller carbon footprint, improved air quality, stormwater management, and biodiversity. Figure 6.2 shows potential streetscape improvement ideas that could be utilized to achieve green density as well as environmental benefits. The illustrated example is a Cluster 5 neighborhood in Phoenix that lacks adequate street trees and sidewalk connectivity. A curbside rain garden could be integrated along the street to increase the pervious surface area, mitigate the negative effects of rainfall, and create a safe buffer between the pedestrian path and car traffic. Interventions of this nature could potentially transform the existing car-oriented street into one that supports mobility for all users. Moreover, illustrated interventions such as bioretention, vegetated swales, and permeable paving could be implemented to optimize the width of existing streets.

DOI: 10.4324/9781003324409-6

Figure 6.1 Examples of green density interventions for redesigning abandoned surface parking and alleyways located in a Cluster 1 neighborhood in Chicago.

Park density makes it possible to accommodate a variety of neighborhood uses and activities, from small pocket parks for intimate neighborhood social gatherings, to larger community parks that can accommodate seasonal farmers' markets. Figure 6.3 shows a Cluster 6 neighborhood in Atlanta that is an example of good park density; it has walkable and bikeable streets as well as convenient access to public transit. Parks in this neighborhood offer dense tree canopies and well-connected streets and sidewalks. It is important to provide park density that is morphologically and functionally integrated with streets and residential blocks—an arrangement that mitigates the problem of neglected open spaces.

Green density can be achieved by redeveloping run-down inner urban post-industrial sites and infrastructures. The Bloomingdale trail in Chicago is an example of a green infrastructure that transformed a derelict railway into an elevated linear park. The trail connects multiple existing neighborhood parks and school yards, and offers 2.7 miles of trail for walking and bicycling (Figure 6.4). This linear green infrastructure integrates dense native plantings along the trail and runs through dense residential areas that provide immediate park access for social integration.

Integrated transit

Urban density has long been part of public transportation planning strategies; density makes it possible to achieve greater transit ridership and is cost-effective. Figure 6.5 illustrates how bus stop locations are integrated with compact residential and commercial development. This is classified

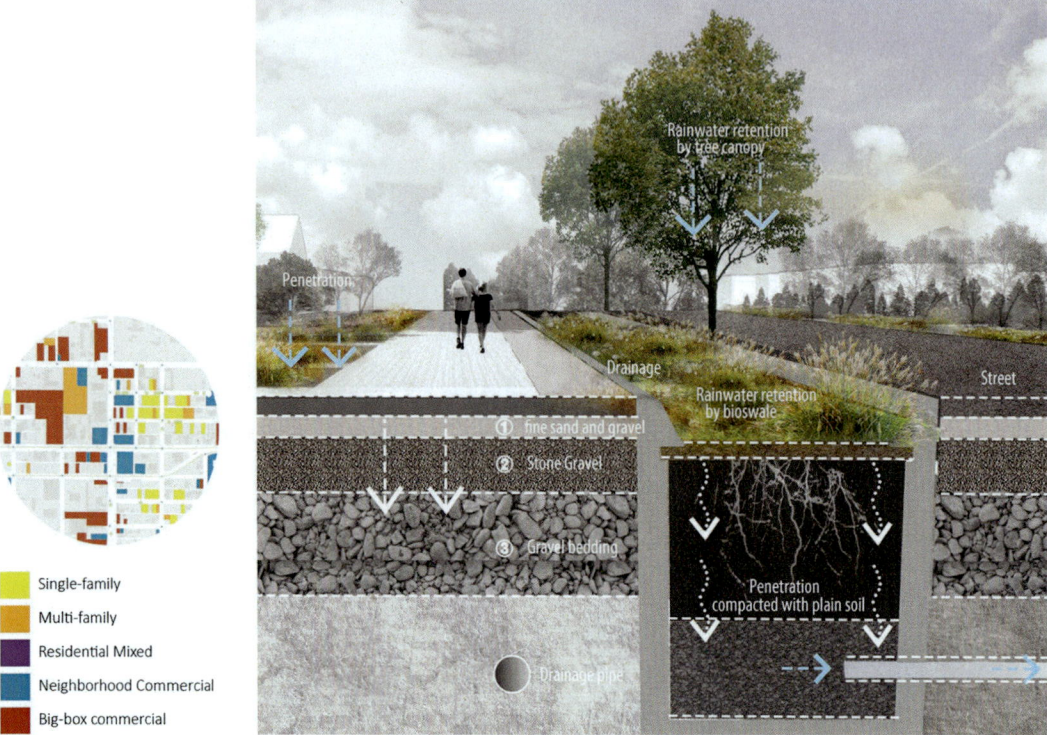

Figure 6.2 Streetscape improvement ideas to achieve green density; an example of Phoenix Cluster 5.

- Single-family
- Multi-family
- Residential Mixed
- Neighborhood Commercial
- Big-box commercial

as a Cluster 6 area in Boston where higher built-form density and population density coexist, as well as various rental and affordable housing options. As seen in this example, integrated transit density offers easy access to public transportation and amenities; it also accommodates low-income families who have limited automobile access.

Land use and zoning regulations should permit residential and commercial density near transportation nodes. Strategies to accomplish this end involve mixed-use development, a variety of affordable housing choices, neighborhood-scale commercial uses that support local economies, and provisions to help residents meet daily needs. Public transit users typically walk a quarter to half a mile to transit stations; locating these amenities along the transit corridor is an arrangement that encourages informal pedestrian street-level activities.

Pedestrian-oriented streetscape design is an important component of transit-supportive density intervention. It engages people in regular, voluntary, and informal street activity which in turn creates safer transit corridors for riders. Additionally, streetscape design should provide dedicated lanes and amenities for micromobility transit, such as bikes, electric scooters, and skateboards. These relatively new and evolving micromobility options offer an alternative transit mode for daily short trips and transit station access.

The integration of green density with transit facilities or corridors generates social and environmental benefits that affect adjacent

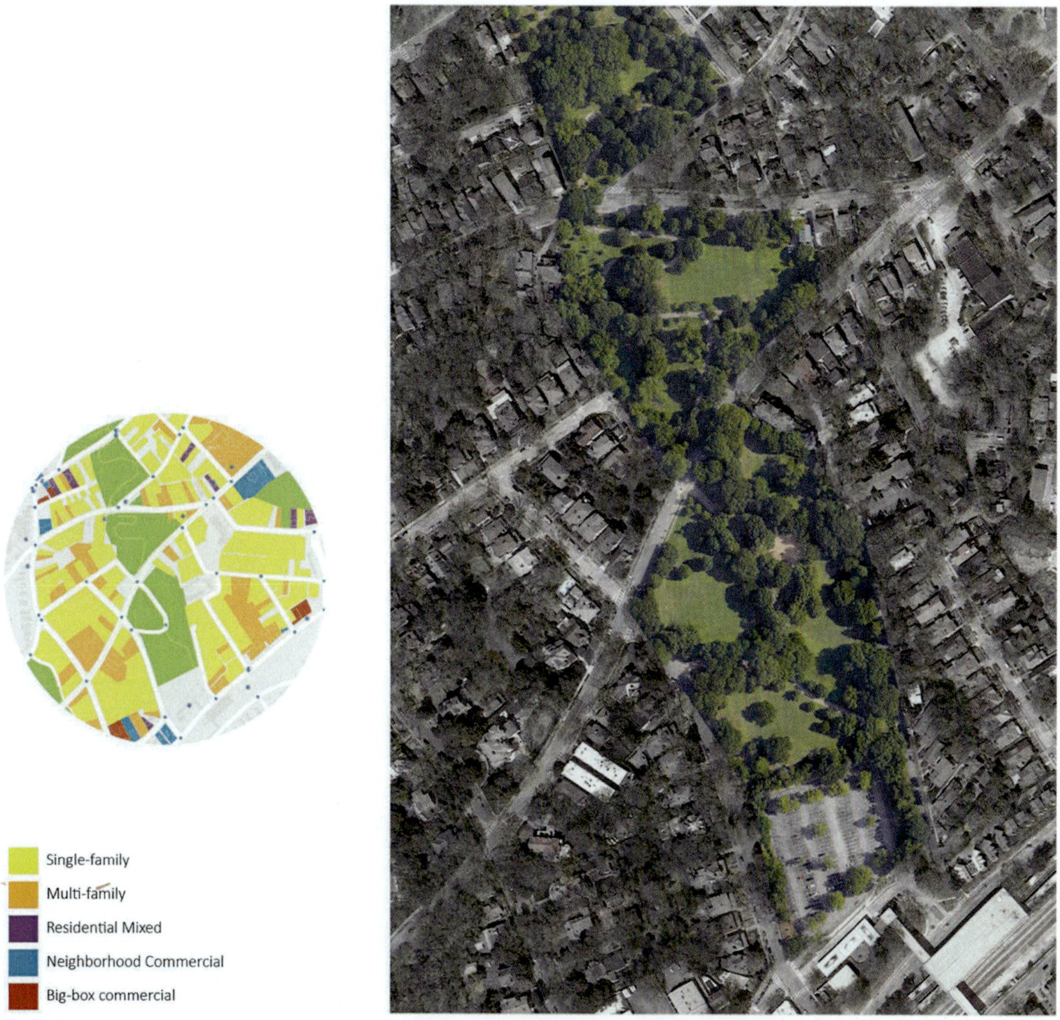

Single-family
Multi-family
Residential Mixed
Neighborhood Commercial
Big-box commercial

Figure 6.3 Park density benefits the adjacent neighborhood; an example of Atlanta Cluster 6.

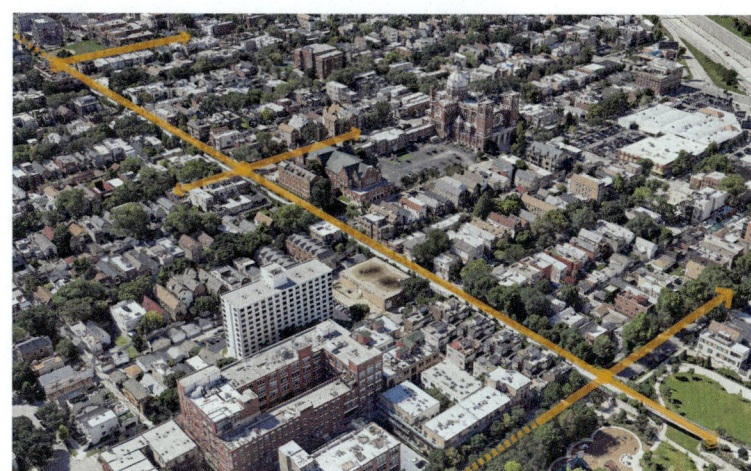

Figure 6.4 An example of neglected railway redevelopment that connects high-density residential blocks; the Bloomingdale Trail in Chicago.

Figure 6.5 Most multifamily residential blocks are covered by transit walk sheds; an example of Boston Cluster 6.

Single-family

Multi-family

Residential Mixed

Neighborhood Commercial

Big-box commercial

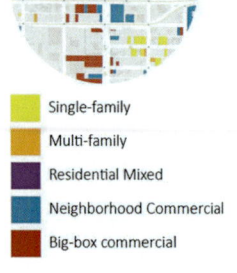

Single-family

Multi-family

Residential Mixed

Neighborhood Commercial

Big-box commercial

Figure 6.6 Small-scale design interventions for better transit experience; an example of Phoenix Cluster 5.

neighborhoods. Although Cluster 5 neighborhoods in Phoenix have relatively good access to bus stops, the accesses are not supported by street trees and other walkable street design features. Figure 6.6 illustrates small-scale design interventions that bring vibrancy to transit experiences. Bus stops with green roofs provide natural elements to streetscapes, retain rainwater, contribute to air quality and micro-scale temperature regulation, and support pollinators. They should be strategically located near parks and community gardens where people can

Figure 6.7 Missing middle housing concept diagram. (missingmiddlehousing.com)

engage in urban farming while commuting—potentially minimizing the impact of food deserts.

Multi-use bus stop design can constitute another strategy to add diverse activities to transit routines. Such small-scale interventions are shown in Figure 6.6: (1) a bus stop library that gives riders access to books they can read while waiting for the bus; and (2) a bus stop mural project that invites local artists to publicly exhibit their creations, thus exposing the community to public art. Interventions of this type can expand a station's purpose and help promote public transit ridership, ultimately helping public transit become more acceptable and integrated into densely developed areas.

Missing middle housing

Missing middle housing (MMH) is a recent movement that promotes housing density by advocating for diverse residential building design strategies. MMH represents the gap between detached single-family homes in lower density neighborhoods and mid-rise multi-family buildings in higher density neighborhoods (Figure 6.7). While critical of current U.S. housing production that focuses on these extreme ends of the density spectrum, the MMH movement stresses the importance of diverse housing types that represent various density forms at different scales.

Figure 6.8 illustrates a Cluster 4 neighborhood land use pattern in Seattle of primarily rental and multi-family housing options. It shows how MMH ideas are implemented and diverse types of *"middle housing"* (from duplex and fourplex, to multi-unit live/work buildings) coexist in the residential area (Figure 6.9). The neighborhood provides diverse housing types for a variety of residential needs while sustaining density, housing affordability, and neighborhood walkability.

Integrating multi-family housing provides various dwelling options beyond detached single-family homes. Figure 6.10 is an example of Cluster 5 in Chicago that illustrates how townhouse and multiplex housing types can be built in single-family neighborhoods. It exemplifies how corner parcels in a block are sufficient to accommodate twin homes as well as multiplex buildings, achieving both greater housing unit and population densities. In addition to benefits related to diverse housing

Figure 6.8 MMH blocks in Cluster 4 neighborhood in Seattle.

- • Intersection
- • Cul-de-sac
- ❀ Grocery store
- Ⓑ Bus stop
- ▉ Tree canopy
- ▉ Parks
- ▉ Single-family
- ▉ Multi-family
- ▉ Residential Mixed
- ▉ Neighborhood Commercial
- ▉ Big-box commercial

opportunities, this strategy stimulates the local economy, as greater population density can potentially attract a broader range of commercial enterprises and other amenities to a neighborhood. Diverse housing options help achieve residential density; they provide a greater number of rental units, smaller homes, and affordable housing choices that attract families of diverse backgrounds.

Figure 6.11 (Cluster 5 in Boston) is a good example of MMH buildings integrated into a single-family residential block in a walkable neighborhood. A neighborhood of this type with greater housing diversity can provide stronger social connections and integration. Resident needs evolve through different phases of life—rental units for young professionals, townhouses for first-time home buyers, downsized options for empty nesters—and residents can remain longer in the same neighborhood when various housing options are available. Moreover, communities with diverse housing options are more resilient in that they are less likely to be affected by foreclosures during a housing market crash (Chakraborty & McMillan, 2022).

Figure 6.12 is another example of MMH in a single-family-oriented neighborhood. Using the Cluster 3 example in Phoenix, the figure visualizes how housing density can be achieved by adding mixed-use, live/work units to a neighborhood primarily consisting of single-family homes and well-maintained streetscapes that support both walking and biking. Integrating live/work units in this neighborhood makes it possible to increase housing unit density as well as provide affordable residential and commercial unit options. It accommodates non-residential uses that provide neighborhood amenities such as local shops and restaurants within walkable proximity to homes. Live/work units can be strategically located close to public amenities such as parks, libraries, and churches, and transport routes to increases accessibility and pedestrian activities.

Figure 6.9 Various multifamily housing options in the Seattle Cluster 4 neighborhood.

Friendly frontage

Integrating friendly frontage design features such as stoops, porches, and front gardens create an attractive building façade and encourage pedestrian activity along the street. With minimized setback distance, it invites lively interactions among those residing in private homes as well as passersby using public spaces. Appropriate building façades and setback distances are important elements of streetscape design when creating walkable and safe streets.

Figure 6.13 is an example of Cluster 3 in Chicago that illustrates a series of porches along the sidewalk that provide semi-public spaces where residents can spontaneously connect and interact. This Cluster 3 neighborhood also depicts a greater degree of rental and affordable housing

Single-family

Multi-family

Residential Mixed

Neighborhood Commercial

Big-box commercial

Figure 6.10 Possible twin homes and townhouse buildings in a single-family neighborhood in Chicago Cluster 5.

density. Integrating small porches into stacked duplex homes not only helps provide places to meet immediate neighbors, they create a shared sense of belonging.

Safe and walkable sidewalks are important components of friendly frontage design integration as well. Front porches and walkable streets collectively encourage vibrant social activities such as informal and spontaneous interactions. Figure 6.14 illustrates a Cluster 1 neighborhood in Seattle that offers single-family homes along with well-connected, safe, and walkable streets. This is another example of a neighborhood with walkable street features that can integrate a friendly frontage strategy to increase social density; it adds another layer of in-between social spaces.

Front porches and stoops are essential parts of building façade design and home extension that impact and define street identity. These

Intersection
Cul-de-sac
Grocery store
Bus stop
Tree canopy
Parks
Single-family
Multi-family
Residential Mixed
Neighborhood Commercial
Big-box commercial

Figure 6.11 Cluster 5 neighborhood in Boston well demonstrates MMH integrated with single-family homes.

transitional spaces allow residents to extend their indoor lifestyle to the semi-public zone and share it with their neighbors. They also reflect residents' culture, history, and identity—allowing them to build community identity collectively.

Communal space

Communal space refers to public space located close to residential blocks that promote positive social interactions. Communal space integrated into multi-family residential buildings offers flexible outdoor areas that play various roles in residents' lives. It can work as an extended living room where residents spend time on their own, a back yard where residents can invite neighbors for informal social gathering, and/or as a safe playground for children.

Figure 6.15 illustrates how a multi-family residential building with communal space can be integrated into a single-family residential neighborhood. The neighborhood is an example of Cluster 4 in Miami mainly involving single-family residential use with low population and housing density. The proposed interventions in Figure 6.15 highlight shared common courtyard-type spaces in a multi-family building. Taking advantage of existing walkable streets, the courtyard that opens to the street welcomes community activities. Parking is located at the rear of the building and each residential unit enters from the shared courtyard.

Figure 6.16 shows how communal space design interventions can be implemented in a multi-family residential complex. The presented neighborhood is classified as Cluster 4 in Atlanta that offers multi-family rental and affordable homes, but it lacks walkability. Its irregular building pattern, community site plan prioritizing parking, and unstructured open space are common morphological characteristics of multi-family subdivisions in the U.S. These undesirable characteristics could be improved by introducing new residential, mixed-use buildings and creating defined open communal spaces on site—a building layout and configuration that would create enclosed external public spaces (Figure 6.17). The change

Figure 6.12 Possible mixed-use, live/work units in Phoenix Cluster 3 neighborhood. These interventions are proposed for sites marked with cross (+).

would better define the block and street network system and provide spatial hierarchy to streets and green open spaces.

Deliberately increasing density around public parks and urban green spaces is an important strategy for making the areas more safe, accessible, and social. Such an approach could destine existing public parks to become more usable communal spaces for nearby residents (Figure 6.3). Research has proven that public parks and green spaces increase economic, environmental, physical, and mental health, in addition to offering social connection benefits to a community. Maintaining residential density around parks makes these benefits attainable for a greater number of residents.

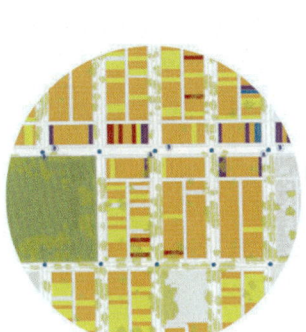 

Figure 6.13 Duplex homes with active frontage in Chicago Cluster 3 neighborhood.

Integrated retail

Neighborhood-scale commercial and retail enterprises that have been integrated into residential areas conveniently provide for the acquisition and satisfaction of daily life needs due to their proximity. Integrated retail units within multi-family residential buildings are particularly useful in that they provide easy accessibility. Figure 6.18 is an exceptionally good example of integrated retail strategies being employed for multi-family and mixed-use development. This neighborhood is classified as Cluster 2 in Chicago with neighborhood-scale commercial density, offering convenient access to grocery stores and other retail units.

Residential areas located near retail are especially important for those living in low-income households and/or have limited mobility and resources. Figure 6.19 is a Cluster 5 neighborhood in Miami consisting of affordable housing with greater unit density, in addition to having a greater number of vacant homes. The figure illustrates how neighborhood-scale retail units can be integrated into residential blocks offering affordable rental options for small business owners. It also positively impacts accessibility and benefits residents with services and amenities located within walking distance. These mixed-use residential buildings can be strategically located adjacent to existing commercial and institutional buildings to create better connectivity and ultimately contribute to improving the sense of neighborhood center.

Figure 6.20 is another example of a neighborhood that illustrates high-density rental and multi-family residential units. This area is classified as Cluster 2 neighborhood in Phoenix with relatively higher population and housing density, and high-vacant unit density with limited access to fresh food and commercial services. The integration of neighborhood-scale retail units is an important strategy—in this case it could

Single-family

Multi-family

Figure 6.14 Front porch design ideas for walkable neighborhoods; Cluster 1 in Seattle.

improve residents' access to daily needs such as groceries. A retail integration strategy could also improve housing unit vacancy. As illustrated in Figure 6.20, convenient access to retailers and other amenities within walking distance offers a desirable living environment, and in turn, it attracts potential residents.

The process of integrating retail units into residential buildings and multi-family housing complexes creates a sense of community-belonging by attracting small business owners, young artists, and creative others together in one area. Live/work spaces and residential-involved mixed-use buildings constitute a common retail space that offers networking opportunities for those in a group to share resources and mutually manage challenges. It also allows retail units to connect directly to

Figure 6.15 Communal space design ideas for a courtyard residential building; Cluster 4 in Miami.

Single-family
Multi-family

the street, becoming social spaces for local residents to engage with their community.

Historic density

Historic density refers to integrated historic design elements that provide historical significance and cultural identity to a community. Figure 6.21 illustrates how historic elements can be integrated into mixed-use development in a post-industrial neighborhood. This is an example of Cluster 6 in Seattle that combines more affordable and vacant housing unit density along with limited walkability. In terms of urban form characteristics, the neighborhoods classified as Seattle Cluster 6 tend to include larger-sized blocks and parcels, lower building density, and a lack of street connectivity. These clusters are generally located adjacent to sites with exceptional spatial patterns and unique identities such as post and current industrial sites, major railway corridors, golf courses, and regional-scale parks (refer to Seattle cluster map in Figure 4.2). Historic density strategies would help these neighborhoods recover their lost identities, enhance their sense of community, and therefore make residential density desirable.

The preservation and restoration of historic building aesthetics help maintain a sense of place and connection to a community's heritage. Figure 6.22 is an example of a historic building restoration that transformed an industrial building into a cafeteria-style market—supporting local vendors and family-owned businesses. The project maintained local characteristics by preserving major historic building design elements within a neighborhood context. It also added environmental sustainability value by repurposing existing structures and reducing construction waste—thus, minimizing negative environmental impact.

Figure 6.16 Communal space design interventions for multifamily residential complex; Cluster 4 in Atlanta.

A historic density strategy provides additional community benefits related to economic sustainability. Retaining the historical character of an area can grow the local economy by attracting visitors and new residents, as well as increasing property values. However, the tenuous relationship between historic preservation and housing affordability caused by gentrification or displacement has caused concern (McCabe & Ellen, 2016). It is important to be aware of the potential challenges historic preservation redevelopment might bring to a neighborhood as changes are made. Redevelopment must leverage historic characteristics as a tool to create affordable housing units by paying close attention to neighborhood characteristics and the potential impact of preservation policies.

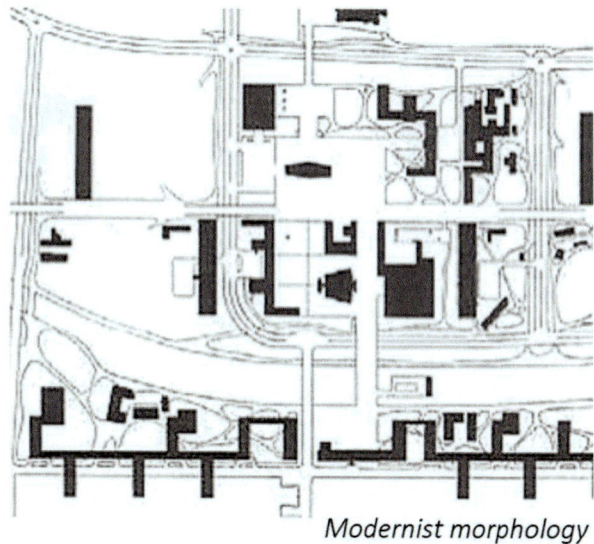

Modernist morphology

Traditional morphology

Figure 6.17 Proposed building layout based on the traditional urban morphology ideas: enclosed communal spaces and streets with hierarchy. In contrast, the modernist morphological approach involves separated freestanding buildings set within super blocks and car-oriented roads (Rowe and Koetter, 1978).

Density as a desirable community value

In this chapter, we reviewed contextual density characteristics of various neighborhoods and proposed urban design interventions that can make density more acceptable and desirable. The main discussion was based on the density assessment reported in Chapter 4 that revealed the current status of complex density characteristics in six major U.S. cities: Atlanta, Boston, Chicago, Miami, Phoenix, and Seattle. The presented urban design strategies illustrated how urban density can be achieved within social norms that are contextually appropriate, culturally acceptable, and environmentally sustainable.

Figure 6.18
Neighborhood-scale
retail integrated into
residential area in
Cluster 2 neighborhood
in Chicago.

- Intersection
- Cul-de-sac
- Grocery store
- Bus stop
- Tree canopy
- Parks
- Single-family
- Multi-family
- Residential Mixed
- Neighborhood Commercial
- Big-box commercial

Figure 6.19 Small retail units integrated into residential blocks can offer affordable rental options for small businesses; Cluster 5 in Miami.

Urban design tactics and strategies have been explored to create positive, dense environments that guarantee equal accessibility. There is a robust relationship between urban density and public transportation development when discussing accessibility. Empirical research supports the idea that higher population and housing density leads to greater ridership and cost-effectiveness of transit development, resulting in a more productive and efficient transit system. Various density strategies, such as increasing housing density and implementing mixed-use development around transit stations, have been suggested to support transit accessibility. These strategies can be implemented by local governments and transit agencies in areas where transit-oriented density guidelines are

Single-family

Multi-family

Residential Mixed

Neighborhood Commercial

Big-box commercial

Figure 6.20 Retail integrated into multifamily residential buildings; Cluster 2 in Phoenix.

needed. This chapter demonstrates various physical design strategies that promote "transportation diversity"—offering various transportation alternatives such as walking, biking, and public transit to enhance access to services and facilities (Talen, 2013, p. 88).

One of the benefits of urban density is its ability to increase accessibility to jobs, promoting employment growth and boosting the local economy (Owens, 1992). Urban density is believed to attract retailers and businesses, as it secures potential customers within the community boundaries. Additionally, urban density is seen as a strategy for increasing collaboration opportunities among people with various skills, as it can maximize social interactions and encounters by bringing people together and creating different job opportunities. This chapter provides examples

Single-family

Multi-family

Residential Mixed

Neighborhood Commercial

Big-box commercial

Figure 6.21 Mixed-use and retail buildings with post-industrial design characteristics; Cluster 6 neighborhood in Seattle.

Figure 6.22 An example of historic building restoration project. The Harris Machine Company building had been located in Minneapolis, MN since 1889 and was redeveloped as a food hall in 2021. (https://makersrow. com/harris-machine-co; https://malcolmyards.market/)

of density strategies that incorporate neighborhood-scale commercial and retail, positively impacting the local economy and job accessibility.

This chapter highlights infill and mixed-use developments as important strategies for increasing urban density. Developing vacant or underused parcels within existing urban areas enhances access to services and facilities. By incorporating a mix of land uses in a neighborhood, the distance between activities is reduced, making it easier for people to access them. The concept of mixed-use is reflected in various density strategies, as it brings commercial activities within walking distance and sustains higher densities than single-use residential areas (Berridge Lewinberg Greenberg, Ltd., 1991). The presented design strategies related to mixed-use and infill developments emphasize how to increase urban density by promoting land-use diversity.

It is believed that higher density provides more opportunities for walking or biking to daily destinations such as work, stores, services, and facilities. Higher built-form density makes it possible to maintain convenient access to those destinations within walking distance from residential areas, which is especially beneficial for individuals with limited mobility and resources, such as low-income families, minority populations, youth, and senior citizens. Researchers have explored various built environment and land use characteristics to understand the relationship between density and walkability. For example, Ewing and Cervero (2010) found that walking is strongly associated with higher intersection diversity, land-use diversity, and a greater number of destinations within walking distance. Additionally, Badland et al. (2008) discovered that street connectivity significantly influences transport-related physical activity behaviors. This chapter presented density strategies that incorporate urban form indicators supporting pedestrians' walkability and accessibility.

Urban density strategies, particularly green density, focus on integrating public parks and street trees to improve residents' quality of life and provide better access to nature. Achieving green space equity is challenging, as it requires fairness and justice in the distribution of public goods and services (Deakin, 1999). Research has shown disparities in the distribution of parks and green spaces among different racial and ethnic groups. For example, neighborhoods predominantly populated by non-White individuals have fewer well-maintained and highly utilized parks (Rigolon, 2016). Moreover, non-White individuals are less likely to enjoy the benefits of local parks and recreation services due to lower park usage (Mowen et al., 2018). Higher green density can lead to better access to urban parks and park equity. It is important to ensure that urban green areas are accessible, inclusive, and meet community needs. In this chapter, we examined how to integrate urban parks and street trees into urban density strategies that can enhance residents' quality of life and create accessible and desirable density characteristics.

The relationship between urban density and safety has been discussed extensively. Density is considered a crucial factor for safe and vibrant social interaction in public settings. Studies have explored how density contributes to creating "eyes on the street," which acts as a form of natural surveillance. Higher population and housing unit density in urban areas tend to generate more foot traffic throughout the day and night, leading to a greater sense of security (Bibri et al., 2020). Green density also influences the sense of safety and security in public spaces and streets. Research indicates that residents' usage of neighborhood parks in low-income areas is closely linked to park proximity, available amenities, and lower reported crime rates (Vaughan et al., 2018). Schusler et al. (2018) found that neighborhoods with a higher degree of tree canopy coverage experience lower crime rates compared to areas with parks alone. This chapter discussed various density interventions as potential strategies to promote neighborhood safety by encouraging informal activities and natural surveillance.

It is believed that urban density fosters a higher level of social interaction and supports more diverse, accessible, and livable living environments. Urban design and planning practices that promote urban density endorse more compact urban forms and patterns, which bring social benefits such as a higher quality of life and social cohesion, as well as environmental and economic benefits such as resource efficiency, protection of rural land, and reduced energy use (Waters, 2016). It is also argued that density addresses issues related to social segregation by enabling a higher level of equal access to services and facilities, thus creating better opportunities for social interaction (Bibri et al., 2020). In this chapter, we suggest that certain density strategies can promote social interaction and reduce social segregation by cultivating positive density characteristics that foster a sense of community and cultural vitality.

Urban density has the potential to provide more affordable housing units, as neighborhoods with greater density are likely to include diverse types of housing design, form, and tenure (Aurand, 2010). This diversity in housing characteristics attracts people with diverse socio-economic backgrounds, potentially meeting the needs of different population groups. It is believed that density promotes social equity by reducing social and spatial segregation through providing diverse housing types, including affordable units, and in turn, better connecting communities (Burton, 2000). However, while population and housing density are appreciated as remedies for social and economic disparity and social inequity, there are criticisms about the market-driven development of multi-family housing in terms of displacement and gentrification. Concerns also exist that this type of development could bring micro-scale segregation while greater density and diversity are observed at a neighborhood-scale. In this chapter, we proposed small-scale design tactics and interventions that help maintain the existing housing diversity and affordability which tackles the challenge of addressing accessibility and affordability together.

This is our exploration of various urban design tactics and strategies based on seven density preference dimensions that are distinct yet interrelated. Design interventions presented in this chapter consider density in conjunction with other urban design values such as walkability, accessibility, connectivity, integration, affordability, and safety. For example, green density interventions are discussed as they relate to walkability and pedestrian safety. Integrated retail strategies are infused with mixed-use development ideas to create better accessibility and potentially offer affordable small business units. Friendly frontage integration is a building design strategy that can make residential density more acceptable while achieving social integration and community identity.

The proposed design interventions in this chapter demonstrate that diverse density possibilities can advance beyond density development regulations based on numeric density assessments alone. Figures 6.23 and 6.24 are examples of high-density residential buildings clustered within a single-use large parcel. These residential buildings are located within superblocks surrounded by redundant open spaces and are segregated by arterial roads. Figure 6.23 shows a suburban neighborhood in Plymouth, MN where high-residential density is achieved, but walkability and accessibility are compromised. Figure 6.24 illustrates another neighborhood in Brooklyn Park, MN where large apartment buildings and single-family homes are located within close proximity; however, the areas are separated by neglected green spaces and wide arterial roads which could potentially lead to a lack of social integration. These examples represent conventional density practices that might impact the publics' opposition to densification.

While urban density contributes to economic, environmental, and social benefits, this type of high-form density with *functional sprawl* is not able to achieve these values; the struggle with lack of walkability, automobile dependency, and weak social and functional integration remains. We hope that the diverse density possibilities presented in this chapter might help contribute to diversifying urban density experiences, and in turn prompt positive attitudes toward density.

Figure 6.23 An example of high residential density with compromised walkability and accessibility (Plymouth, MN).

Figure 6.24 An example
of high residential
density surrounded by
redundant open spaces
and arterial roads
(Brooklyn Park, MN).

Literature cited

Aurand, A. (2010). Density, housing types and mixed land use: Smart tools for
affordable housing? *Urban Studies*, *47*(5), 1015–1036.

Badland, H. M., Schofield, G. M., & Garrett, N. (2008). Travel behavior and
objectively measured urban design variables: Associations for adults traveling
to work. *Health & Place*, *14*(1), 85–95.

Berridge Lewinberg Greenberg, Ltd. (1991). *Guidelines for the reurbanisation
of Metropolitan Toronto*. Toronto: Municipality of Metropolitan Toronto
Corporate Printing Services.

Bibri, S. E., Krogstie, J., & Kärrholm, M. (2020). Compact city planning and
development: Emerging practices and strategies for achieving the goals of
sustainability. *Developments in the Built Environment*, *4*, 100021.

Burton, E. (2000). The compact city: Just or just compact? A preliminary analysis.
Urban Studies, *37*(11), 1969–2006.

Chakraborty, A., & McMillan, A. (2022). Is housing diversity good for community
stability? Evidence from the housing crisis. *Journal of Planning Education and
Research*, *42*(2), 150–161.

Deakin, E. (1999). Social equity in planning. *Berkeley Planning Journal*, *13*(1), 1–5.

Ewing, R., & Cervero, R. (2010). Travel and the built environment. *Journal of the
American Planning Association*, *76*, 265–294.

McCabe, B. J., & Ellen, I. G. (2016). Does preservation accelerate neighborhood
change? Examining the impact of historic preservation in New York City.
Journal of the American Planning Association, *82*(2), 134–146. https://doi.org/
10.1080/01944363.2015.1126195.

Mowen, A. J., Barrett, A., Pitas, N., Graefe, A. R., Taff, B. D., & Godbey, G. (2018).
Americans' use and perceptions of local park and recreation services: Results
from an updated study. *Journal of Park and Recreation Administration*, *36*(4),
128–148.

Owens, S. (1992). Energy, environmental sustainability and land-use planning.
Sustainable Development and Urban Form, *2*, 79–105.

Rigolon, A. (2016). A complex landscape of inequity in access to urban parks:
A literature review. *Landscape and Urban Olanning*, *153*, 160–169.

Schusler, T., Weiss, L., Treering, D., & Balderama, E. (2018). Research note: Examining the association between tree canopy, parks and crime in Chicago. *Landscape and Urban Planning*, *170*, 309–313.

Talen, E. (2013). Prospects for walkable, mixed-income neighborhoods: Insights from US developers. *Journal of Housing and the Built Environment*, *28*, 79–94.

Vaughan, C. A., Colabianchi, N., Hunter, G. P., Beckman, R., & Dubowitz, T. (2018). Park use in low-income urban neighborhoods: Who uses the parks and why? *Journal of Urban Health*, *95*, 222–231.

Waters, J. (2016). *Accessible cities: From urban density to multidimensional accessibility. In Rethinking sustainable cities* (pp. 11–60). Chicago, IL: Policy Press.

7

CONCLUSION

Density as it relates to city planning must be well understood because of its implications for sustainability, livability, as well as social justice. Due to its complex and paradoxical nature, it can also be controversial—not everyone is on board with what density has to offer. There is wide agreement that density is not merely a numerical measure; it is a critical factor in fostering sustainable, vibrant, and socially connected cities. However, density is often misunderstood and misrepresented, leading to ongoing challenges in urban planning and policy-making. What is needed–and what we have tried to provide in this book—is a more nuanced understanding of density. We have tried to achieve this nuance by exploring the contextual characteristics and variations of density as well as proposing actionable strategies for living closer together in urban spaces.

We believe that much of the misunderstanding about density is related to its design and context—both of which can be controlled where there is political will. The density that has been created in un-serviced areas lacking transit options is not a form of density that will reap benefits. Ultimately, it will undermine residents' ability to see the value of density as well.

In this book, we have attempted to unravel these issues by presenting a comprehensive exploration of urban density, delving into its multifaceted dimensions and contextual implications. Case studies and empirical analyses have been used to illuminate the complex relationships that define and shape the concept of density in its various urban environments.

We began with a brief history of density which was derided a century ago, and yet subsequently viewed as essential. We showed how the same five dimensions that were used to demonize density—public health and safety, commute choices, housing affordability, property owner preference, and environmental concern—were the same five dimensions used later in a higher valuation of density. This has been borne out in recent decades by an increased understanding that density is essential for walkable, sustainable, and pedestrian-oriented urbanism.

In Chapter 2, we analyze the concept of density in three typical U.S. settings, exploring its implications and potential interpretations. We examine various density examples from the City of Chicago, comparing two variations of "housing in a park"—multi-family housing and single-family detached housing in a suburban setting—with "old urbanism," which refers to older urban housing in traditional urban neighborhoods. The argument

DOI: 10.4324/9781003324409-7

is made that these three density contexts offer distinct experiences and carry different meanings and implications.

In Chapter 3, we used the city of Chicago as a case study to investigate whether density makes sense in terms of spatial patterning—based on the idea that density and urban amenities should be co-located; and furthermore, that this co-location will sustain an urban quality of life. How, we wondered, do different density types relate locationally to park, transit, and other service accesses? Our analysis revealed that the relationship between density and urban amenities is complex and often counterintuitive. For instance, while higher density was expected to correlate with better access to parks and transit, the data showed mixed results. This chapter underscored the importance of considering spatial patterns and local context when evaluating the benefits and challenges of urban density.

We further analyzed density in Chapter 4: we attempted to validate claims about the relationship between urban density and various amenities by investigating the multi-dimensional aspects of density. We considered how density is a descriptive, normative, and relational concept—frequently measured by population numbers, housing units, and buildings—that often ignores how density is related to the spatial, environmental, and functional characteristics of a city. The methodology we developed created a typology for six cities: Atlanta, Boston, Chicago, Miami, Phoenix, and Seattle. We subsequently analyzed 26 variables organized into five groups that could differentiate density: population and housing density; built-form density; walkable street density; land use density; and service and facility density. After exploring the relationships among these 26 density measures using factor analysis, we used cluster analysis to reveal the density typology contexts for each city. The goal was to demonstrate an alternative density assessment method that could reflect the multi-dimensional characteristics of density in spatial, environmental, and functional contexts. The results showed how these density dimensions do not align in a linear way; one type of density in a given location can be high, while another type can be low. Each city displayed a different pattern and a different set of relationships. We found a complex relationship existing between urban density and its spatial patterns, confirming that traditional density measures do not always align with experiential density.

Chapter 5 was devoted to understanding density preferences, and the results of a visual survey of 186 respondents was presented. We introduced seven key components of density—green density, integrated transit, missing middle housing, friendly frontage, communal space, integrated retail, and historic density—and used our survey to both understand the strength of these dimensions and to determine whether they contribute to density acceptance. We also asked respondents to tell us about their socioeconomic backgrounds and current living environments, finding that their current housing and living environment did seem to matter. Somewhat predictably, those currently living in single-family detached housing or in small towns and rural areas were the respondents least likely to feel positive about density overall. But, a majority of all respondents, regardless of their current living environment, had a positive view of density if it showed green density, missing middle, friendly frontage, historic architecture, or communal space. This bodes well for the notion that it is possible to find ways to build density which appeal to a large range of individuals.

This chapter emphasized the importance of viewing density as a multifaceted concept that involves more than population numbers or housing units. By considering contextual factors such as green space, social interaction, and historic architecture, we can better understand what creates preferred density. Ultimately, we can develop density strategies that both increase the number of people living in urban areas *and* enhance the quality of urban life.

Finally, Chapter 6 brought the theoretical discussions of previous chapters into the real world by examining how density strategies have been implemented in various cities. Through a series of case studies, this chapter explored successful examples of urban density in differing contexts, such as high-density housing developments, integrated transit corridors, and green infrastructure projects. Each case study illustrated how density can be adapted to meet the unique needs and characteristics of particular urban areas, offering valuable lessons for cities seeking to increase density in ways that are both effective and contextually appropriate. This chapter stresses that there is no one-size-fits-all solution to urban density, and that successful implementation requires careful consideration of local conditions and community goals.

The case studies presented in Chapter 6 serve as a reminder that successful density strategies are those tailored to the specific conditions of each city or neighborhood. Whether it is integrating green infrastructure into dense urban areas, promoting TOD, or preserving local identity through historic density, the key is to adapt strategies that fit unique contexts. This approach not only ensures that density contributes to urban vitality, it also helps to build stronger and more connected communities.

One of the key takeaways from this book is the importance of moving beyond traditional, one-dimensional approaches to density. Simply increasing the number of people or housing units in an area is not enough, nor is it necessarily preferable from a sustainability standpoint. Instead, there is a need to consider how density interacts with other factors, such as zoning, transit, green space, and social infrastructure to create environments that are truly livable and resilient. This requires a shift in how we think about and measure density—moving from a purely quantitative perspective to one that is more qualitative and contextually sensitive. To achieve density that is contextually appropriate, culturally acceptable, and environmentally sustainable, we suggest that the following aspects need to be considered for contextual density assessments and implications:

1. *Human scale*: Human scale refers to human behavioral and experiential dimensions that are important factors in the achievement of positive experiential density. It refers to smaller morphological and functional components of the environment that impact human

sensory stimuli in relation to interaction with others and experience in urban spaces. Urban density development based on a sense of human scale allows people to respond better to their surroundings and provides more opportunities for social interactions. It also stresses the importance of incremental changes that can potentially accommodate the public components of everyday life in public spaces.

Strategies for urban density based on the human scale focus on how people interact with streets and parks in urban areas. These strategies emphasize the design of streetscapes, including improvements to sidewalks, street lighting, landscape design, and accessible public transport stops, all aimed at enhancing the pedestrian experience. Small-scale design interventions, such as creating community gardens in underutilized alleyways, can support various neighborhood activities. Additionally, implementing small-scale environmental design interventions like bioretention, vegetated swales, and permeable paving can bring environmental benefits to densely populated neighborhoods.

Integrating design features of friendly frontage is one of the implications of human scale that encourages pedestrian activity. Porches, stoops, and front gardens not only create an attractive building facade but also promote interactions among residents and passersby. These features allow people to extend their indoor life and share it with their neighbors, creating a sense of community and livelihood. It is important to pay attention to building setback distances and create a welcoming frontage strategy to enhance social density. This form of human-scale design tactics aims to create pedestrian-friendly and safe streets and provide additional in-between social spaces.

2. *Walkable and accessible environment*: Well-connected streets and sidewalks are major elements of successful neighborhood walkability that influence walking experiences and destination routes. A strong relationship between walkability and a dense development pattern provides convenient access to services and amenities. The distance between home and various utilitarian destinations (grocery stores, schools, coffee shops, parks, libraries, etc.) is important to consider when determining whether residents feel confident walking to them, and density is the factor that makes it possible to achieve a high level of neighborhood walkability and accessibility.

Integrating retail units into residential areas has several benefits, including improving neighborhood walkability and accessibility. This integration emphasizes the convenience of having retail services nearby for daily needs. It is particularly important for low-income households and individuals with limited mobility, as it can provide essential services and amenities within walking distance. Assessing walkability and accessibility at a neighborhood scale can help maintain density and reduce housing vacancy. Introducing local retail spaces is an important strategy as it can improve access to fresh food and commercial services. Considering residents' access to retailers and amenities within walking distance can positively impact housing vacancy by creating an attractive living environment and drawing potential residents.

Assessing walkability and accessibility is crucial for integrating public transit into density strategies. Designing streetscapes that prioritize pedestrians is essential for increasing the density of transit-friendly areas. This encourages people to engage in various activities on the streets, ultimately leading to the creation of safer transit routes for passengers. Appropriately locating transit stops and ensuring they are accessible from compact residential and commercial developments can provide easy access to public transportation and amenities, better accommodating residents with limited automobile access.

3. *Diverse housing choices*: Diverse housing types along with higher density development invite residents from diverse socio-cultural backgrounds, and various lot shapes and sizes contribute to the promotion of housing type diversity as well. The wide range of housing diversity involved renders it essential to consider in terms of tenure, size, age of buildings, and affordability to accommodate residential needs.

   Neighborhoods with diverse housing choices help maintain housing density and affordability by offering a range of residential options such as duplexes, fourplexes, and multi-unit live/work buildings. This concept is related to the MMH movement, which aims to increase housing unit density by encouraging diverse residential building types. The focus is on filling the gap between single-family homes in low-density neighborhoods and mid-rise multi-family buildings in high-density neighborhoods. This strategy can benefit the local economy by attracting a wider range of commercial enterprises and amenities to the neighborhood. Additionally, this housing diversity strategy can lead to stronger social connections and integration, while meeting the evolving needs of residents at different stages of life.

   Diverse housing choices that incorporate multi-family residential buildings and mixed-use buildings offer shared communal spaces on site, promoting positive social interactions. These spaces can function as an extension of residents' homes, providing a venue for informal gatherings and a safe area for children to play. Additionally, the design of courtyard buildings and cottage courts leads to a greater number of housing units while providing shared communal spaces that open to the street and offer more usable outdoor areas for larger community activities.

4. *Zoning flexibility*: It is important to integrate flexible zoning that allows for higher density development; such zones must align with existing contextual characteristics. Current zoning practices often hinder the development of higher density, mixed-use environments by imposing numeric density parameters and regulations. Reforms that allow for more flexible and contextually appropriate zoning can help cities achieve the benefits of density while avoiding the pitfalls of under-serviced housing and environmental degradation.

   The regulation and evaluation of density often involve land-use restrictions, floor area ratios, and housing unit limits. This highlights the limitations of traditional zoning, which enforces numeric density regulations. In order to consider the social and functional aspects of contextual density, zoning reforms play a significant role in understanding contextual density characteristics that represent local preferences and identities. The implementation of density strategies hinges on the support of zoning reforms to facilitate the creation of a wider range of appealing and desirable density options.

The implications of historic density strategies, such as historic building preservation and post-industrial neighborhood revitalization, can be positively impacted by zoning reforms. Land use and zoning regulations should allow for residential and commercial density near transportation hubs. Zoning reforms make it possible to achieve mixed-use development, providing various affordable housing options and integrating neighborhood-scale commercial activities along transit corridors. A critical first step to reforming zoning is to permit various types of multi-family residential buildings within lower density neighborhoods. In order to integrate local retail units in residential areas, flexible zoning is key to allowing mixed-use buildings and blocks and creating better access to fresh food and commercial services for residents. Zoning that allows flexible building design requirements facilitates minimized setback distance and friendly frontage design features, impacting the creation of walkable and safe streets.

We hope this book will provide a framework for urban planners and policymakers to help them think about density in a more holistic and integrated manner—when it comes to density, context is king. The collective insights presented in these chapters point to a crucial understanding about density: when thoughtfully planned and contextually applied, urban density can be a powerful tool for creating more sustainable, equitable, and vibrant cities.

We hope to have also made the case that the relationship between density and urban quality is not straightforward. Higher density does not automatically lead to better access to parks, greater accessibility to transit, or improved affordability—although it certainly should. But, because of these complications, density must be integrated into urban planning with a clear understanding of context and spatial pattern.

This book has aimed to provide a nuanced understanding of urban density in context, challenging traditional assumptions and offering new perspectives on how density can be used to create better cities. The findings presented in this book should be used to pursue density not as an end in itself, but as a means to achieve broader urban goals such as sustainability, equity, and social connection. By taking a more nuanced and contextually aware approach to density, urban planners, policymakers, and communities can work together to build cities that are not just densely populated, but are ultimately more livable, resilient, and inclusive.

Index

Note: **Bold** page numbers refer to tables; *italic* page numbers refer to figures and page numbers followed by "n" denote endnotes.

Printed in the United States
by Baker & Taylor Publisher Services